LEAKED SECRET TRANSCRIPTS FROM BUSH'S OVAL OFFICE, 2002-2004

By Lee Waters

CICJ Books

LEAKED SECRET TRANSCRIPTS
FROM BUSH'S OVAL OFFICE, 2002-2004
By Lee Waters

Copyright © 2004 by Lee Waters & the Columbus Institute for Contemporary Journalism

CICJ Books: freepress.org
The CICJ is a 501(C)3 Organization
1240 Bryden Road; Columbus, Ohio 43205

ISBN 0-9753402-7-1

This publication is satire. Any relationship to actual White House meetings is merely an educated guess and highly unfortunate.

```
LEAKED SECRET TRANSCRIPTS FROM
BUSH'S OVAL OFFICE, 2002-2004
```

CONTENTS:

Part One: THAT SONOFABITCH TRIED TO KILL MY DADDY

2002, November	"Let's roll, Turdblossom"
2002, December	"That ChickenHawk thing"
2002, December	"All those liberals soiling themselves"
2002, Christmas	"It cost good money to cut the balls off the Democratic Party"
2003, New Years	"It's right here in Revelations"
2003, January	"They're all going to prison, Colin"
2003, February	"Armageddon is overdue"
2003, Valentine's	"Terrorism is the health of the state"
2003, March	"Democracy is for wimps"
2003, March	"War is peace"

PART TWO: MISSION ACCOMPLISHED

2003, April	"We have brought democracy to Iraq"
2003, May	"Mission accomplished, George"
2003, June	"There IS no rest of the world"
2003, July	"I want my flight suit"
2003, August	"George will run as a Peace Candidate"
2003, August	"We kicked their butts in Vietnam"
2003, August	"Focused Democrats are known terrorists"
2003, September	"Arnold's Three Commandments"

PART THREE: OSAMA IN OCTOBER

2004, January	"You've got to push the button!"
2004, February	"Osama in October"
2004, March	"The Democrats even begin to think they can beat us"
2004, March	"Better bone up on your Cuban"
2004, April	"Tony! Tony! Tony!"
2004, May	"Dancing in the streets of Fellatio"
2004, June	"Kerry is still too damn tall"
2004, August	"It's the Apocalypse! Now!!!"

PART ONE: THAT SONOFABITCH TRIED TO KILL MY DADDY

ONE: November, 2002
"Let's roll, Turdblossom"

PRESIDENT BUSH: Good morning, Turdblossom.

KARL ROVE: I wish you wouldn't call me that, George.

PRESIDENT BUSH: Hey, you just pulled off the total take-over of the United States government. Thanks to the great Boy Genius---that's you, Karl---we now control the United States Senate, the House, the Supreme Court, the White House, the Media and the corporate structure. Can I use the D word?

VICE PRESIDENT CHENEY: Would that be Dictator? Or Dick Cheney? Ha ha ha.

KARL ROVE: It's now November, 2002. I say by November, 2004 there will no Democratic Party, no liberal media, no Bill of Rights, none of that bullshit.

VICE-PRESIDENT CHENEY: They can all go fuck themselves.

SECRETARY RUMSFELD: We can finally plan for canceling the 2004 elections.

ATTORNEY-GENERAL ASHCROFT: Demanding national elections is an act of terrorism.

PRESIDENT BUSH: Let's roll, Turdblossom!!!!

KARL ROVE: Can you stop calling me that?

VICE PRESIDENT CHENEY: How about we celebrate by sending some more anthrax to that asshole Pat Leahy.

PRESIDENT BUSH: Yeah, and Tommy Daschle, too. What wimps.

KARL ROVE: Nobody's gonna stop us now.

ATTORNEY-GENERAL ASHCROFT: Opposing the Administration of George W. Bush is an act of terrorism. Mind if I sing?

SECRETARY RUMSFELD: You're either with us, or you're with the terrorists.

PRESIDENT BUSH: John, hold the songs for now, will you? I just ate.

VICE PRESIDENT CHENEY: You did a great job, Karl. But this election was a lot closer than we wanted, even for a mid-term. Rubbing out Paul Wellstone was not originally in the game plan.

KARL ROVE: Extraordinary times demand extraordinary courage. We also had to rough up Max Cleland down in Georgia.

VICE PRESIDENT CHENEY: Well, yeah, but we didn't kill him.

KARL ROVE: We were ready. It proved unnecessary.

PRESIDENT BUSH: Do you realize that if it wasn't for the plane crashes that killed Paul Wellstone and Mel Carnahan the heathen Democrats would still control the US Senate? How lucky can we get?

ALL: *Loud, prolonged laughter.*

ATTORNEY-GENERAL ASHCROFT: The Good Lord gives us leave to rid the planet of those who would stand in our way. Praise Jesus.

SECRETARY RIDGE: Mel Carnahan was leading John here in 2000 in Missouri when he died in a plane crash just prior to the election. Paul Wellstone was set to win a third term in 2002 in Minnesota when he died in a plane crash just prior to the election.

PRESIDENT BUSH: That loser Al Gore has been spouting off lately. We fucked him fair and square and now he's whining about it.

VICE PRESIDENT CHENEY: He belongs on a Wellstone Express.

SECRETARY RUMSFELD: I'm not sure that would be such a good idea. After Carnahan and Wellstone another private plane crash might seem a bit obvious.

PRESIDENT BUSH: Hell, we just missed getting Teddy Kennedy on that plane with Wellstone. Who knows who we might take down with Gore. Maybe even John Kerry.

KARL ROVE: Tom, we can kill every whiny liberal atheist we want and nobody's gonna say a word. One phone call to Roger Ailes at Fox or Rush or Hannity or O'Reilly and every death in America can be blamed on Osama bin Laden or Saddam Hussein. This is REAL POWER! .

ATTORNEY-GENERAL ASHCROFT: Praise the Lord!

PRESIDENT BUSH: I told you to lay off Osama, Karl. My family's been doing business with his for a long, long time and we intend to keep on doing it. We owe him an awful lot for September 11 and don't you forget it. Why do you think we hustled his family out of here after they hit World Trade Center?

KARL ROVE: Right George. Sorry.

PRESIDENT BUSH: I want Saddam dead. That towel-headed sonofabitch tried to kill my Daddy. That don't fly in Texas.

KARL ROVE: We've been honing the neo-con plan to attack Iraq for ten years. September 11 was just the cover we needed. The time is just about right.

PRESIDENT BUSH: I'm tired of pussyfootin' around. What are we, Democrats?

SECRETARY POWELL: Europe isn't buying into an attack on Iraq. They don't believe Saddam has Weapons of Mass Destruction. They don't think he did September 11.

VICE PRESIDENT CHENEY: The poll numbers we cooked up here are pretty good. But I'm not sure they'll hold once the body bags start coming home.

SECRETARY RUMSFELD: Nobody's gonna see the goddam body bags.

PRESIDENT BUSH: We don't need Europe. We don't need NATO. We don't need the United Nations.

SECRETARY RUMSFELD: Fuck em all. Lets just nuke Iraq and get it over with.

VICE PRESIDENT CHENEY: We can't nuke all that oil, Don.

KARL ROVE: Remember the plan? We used the war hype to divert the Democrats from domestic issues and hand us the 2002 mid-term elections. Daschle and those other DLC wimps just groveled at our feet. It was almost embarrassing.

VICE PRESIDENT CHENEY: For 2004 we need gas prices down. We need that sweet Iraqi oil to flood the market and outflank OPEC.

KARL ROVE: Oil prices are the surest indicator of who wins a presidential election.

SECRETARY RUMSFELD: Likewise the gas from that pipeline we're shoving across Afghanistan.

KARL ROVE: Right. Gas down ten cents by November, 2004, and we win. Then it's REALLY all over.

PRESIDENT BUSH: These elections are a damn pain in the ass. And I'm not sure Jeb's gonna deliver this time. Last time, Mom made him.

VICE PRESIDENT CHENEY: If that fourth 9/11 jet had hit Congress, this would all be a lot easier. Who knew the passengers would bring it down in Pennsylvania?

PRESIDENT BUSH: I heard one of those guys was gay.

VICE PRESIDENT CHENEY: It would've been beautiful to see that plane fly into the Congressional dome. Our cameras in the bunker were all focused on it.

KARL ROVE: We're all glad you were so comfortably hidden, Dick. We may set up permanent offices in that bunker as we consolidate the final take-over.

ATTORNEY-GENERAL ASHCROFT: The worship facilities are wonderful. Like the ancient catacombs. Praise Jesus.

PRESIDENT BUSH: I've got a tee time. We meet again in a week.

TWO: DECEMBER, 2002
"That ChickenHawk thing"

PRESIDENT BUSH: Good morning, Gentlemen.

KARL ROVE: Hello, George.

VICE PRESIDENT CHENEY: It's beginning to sink in. I like it.

PRESIDENT BUSH: What's that, Dick?

VICE PRESIDENT CHENEY: Absolute power. The Democrats, the media, the courts. They're all beginning to understand that since the mid-term election, we now totally rule this country.

SECRETARY RUMSFELD: And thus the world. Lets attack Iraq.

ATTORNEY-GENERAL ASHCROFT: It's the will of God. We are elected by the Lord. Jesus is coming. May I sing?

PRESIDENT BUSH: I went to church yesterday. They sang there.

KARL ROVE: We still have the election of 2004 to get through. You read the voting machine memo, yes Tom?

SECRETARY RIDGE: Yes sir, I found it very disturbing.

VICE PRESIDENT CHENEY: You're not going limp on us, are you Tom?

SECRETARY RIDGE: No no. It just never occurred to me how easily we could take over this country. Why didn't we do it under Reagan? Or George's father?

VICE PRESIDENT CHENEY: Nancy got in the way. Then Poppy ran out of time. Got distracted by Saddam. Didn't take care of business.

PRESIDENT BUSH: We'll take care of Saddam this time. When do we attack?

KARL ROVE: By November, 2004, we want every precinct in America to have an electronic voting machine. Wally O'Dell at Diebold has it all wired. Homeland Security will have the code to every one of those machines.

VICE PRESIDENT CHENEY: The election of 2004 will be decided by a few keystrokes at Homeland Security.

PRESIDENT BUSH: Sounds right to me. Who's gonna win?

ALL: *Loud, prolonged laughter.*

VICE PRESIDENT CHENEY: We can't have another Florida 2000. All those butterfly ballots and hanging chads. It was bad PR.

KARL ROVE: It dragged on too damn long. Then that Harris woman….

VICE PRESIDENT CHENEY: The chair of the Bush for President campaign in Florida was in charge of counting the votes for the state. Can we be a little more subtle next time?

SECRETARY RUMSFELD: Why not just march in the goddam troops and take over?

VICE PRESIDENT CHENEY: I did love all those Jews voting for Pat Buchanan. A very cute touch, Karl. It's important in this business to have a sense of humor. That's why I'm always photographed smiling. Ha ha ha.

KARL ROVE: Well, we didn't exactly plan that Buchanan thing. We just got lucky.

ATTORNEY-GENERAL ASHCROFT: It was the will of God!!! (singing) *Aaaamazing grace, how…*

PRESIDENT BUSH: Shut up, John.

KARL ROVE: We figured getting Katherine Harris to knock off all those black Democrats with the no votes for felons law would do it for us. We were right. .

SECRETARY RIDGE: Banning felons from voting was a law passed by racist Democrats in the former Confederacy after the Civil War. It was meant to keep freed slaves from voting. They threw in a few well-placed lynchings.

SECRETARY RUMSFELD: Very effective.

KARL ROVE: It worked again for us in Florida in 2000. And in some other states we don't talk about.

VICE PRESIDENT CHENEY: I hate to say it, but they really did kick our butts. Florida, West Virginia, Tennessee, Arkansas. Thank God for voter fraud.

PRESIDENT BUSH: Ashcroft, before you break into song, let me say it for you: We have been chosen by God. That's the opposite of Dog.

VICE PRESIDENT CHENEY: Well, we certainly weren't elected by the American people. But who gives a shit. We've got the power. What else matters?

SECRETARY RIDGE: So you can get the programming for all the voting machines in the country. And you want us at Homeland Security to rig the election?

PRESIDENT BUSH: Sounds good to me.

SECRETARY RIDGE: And how do you plan to keep this all secret?

VICE PRESIDENT CHENEY: We don't. Our media will just make it look like another kooky leftist conspiracy theory.

KARL ROVE: Rush has his talking points. And O'Reilly. And Ann Coulter. The usual suspects. Just let the left try to run with this one. We'll cut them to pieces.

SECRETARY RIDGE: Are you sure you can steal another election? People are still upset about 2000.

VICE PRESIDENT CHENEY: For the past 150 years white politicians have been knocking anywhere from 5 to 25% off inner city vote counts. "Spoiled ballots."

ATTORNEY-GENERAL ASHCROFT: The will of God has saved the nation from heathens and Communists. .

VICE PRESIDENT CHENEY: The Will of God and voter fraud. Ha ha ha.

KARL ROVE: We learned in 2000 it's tough to shred all those paper ballots and turn away those black voters. So in 2004, Homeland Security will do it all with a few keystrokes.

SECRETARY RIDGE: I'm not sure….

KARL ROVE: The software that runs the voting machines is controlled by three big companies, all tied to Diebold. All in our pocket. We keep that code very private. But on election day, Homeland Security will make sure the right party wins. Simple as that.

SECRETARY RUMSFELD: It's like what Joe Stalin said: it doesn't matter who casts the votes, only who counts them. He was a hell of a guy.

VICE PRESIDENT CHENEY: Those bleeding heart Jimmy Carter liberals can make sure everybody votes. Just as long as they can't read computer code.

KARL ROVE: And Tom sits at Homeland Security with your black boxes and watches where it gets too close. And then make it un-close. Got it?

SECRETARY RUMSFELD: Yeah, let those blacks and Jews and Hispanics and femi-nazis and gays vote to their heart's content. It's their Constitutional right. But nothing in the Constitution says we actually gotta COUNT those votes.

SECRETARY RIDGE: But what about the ACLU? And all those people campaigning for voting machine paper trails?

ATTORNEY-GENERAL ASHCROFT: Demanding a paper ballot is an act of terrorism.

VICE PRESIDENT CHENEY: Starting with the USA PATRIOT Act and all the other legislation we've given you, we can arrest or shoot pretty much anyone we want.

SECRETARY RUMSFELD: Arrest 'em if you can. Whack 'em if you have to.

SECRETARY RIDGE: Whack 'em?

KARL ROVE: Like Wellstone. Like Carnahan. Don't you realize if we hadn't taken those two out the Senate might still be in heathen hands?

PRESIDENT BUSH: And Cleland. Don't forget Cleland.

KARL ROVE: If we hadn't been sure the computer voting machines in that Georgia Senate race could be rigged, we might have had to do to Cleland what we did to Wellstone. So in a very real sense, the technology saved Max's life.

ATTORNEY-GENERAL ASHCROFT: Hallelujah!

PRESIDENT BUSH: But you guys are missing the other thing Tom's gotta do here. That ChickenHawk thing.

VICE PRESIDENT CHENEY: George, you're overly sensitive. Just because Max Cleland fought in Vietnam and none of us did means nothing.

SECRETARY RUMSFELD: We already know you had "other priorities," Dick. But George's Guard records ain't pretty.

KARL ROVE: By contrast, we've smeared Max Cleland's patriotism. And we've fed Ann Coulter some good stuff about how he got blown up over there.

SECRETARY RUMSFELD: Oh, that's brilliant Karl. Ann Coulter attacking Max Cleland. Did she get her purple heart in the culture war?

KARL ROVE: What we proved in Georgia 2002 was that it's possible to attack the patriotism of an acknowledged war hero, even one who lost three limbs. It's possible to beat that war hero with a candidate who never went to war himself. All you need is a big TV budget, a few smear ads, and control of the voting machines.

VICE PRESIDENT CHENEY: We shoved Max Cleland's war medals right up his…

PRESIDENT BUSH: It's that ChickenHawk thing I don't like.

SECRETARY RIDGE: You mean the reference to the fact that the leaders of this administration all avoided service to their country?

SECRETARY POWELL: Watch your mouth, fella.

PRESIDENT BUSH: I want your computers to watch for that damn word. That ChickenHawk word. I don't like it.

SECRETARY RIDGE: What shall I do, Mr. President?

VICE PRESIDENT CHENEY: Set your scanners, Tom. Whoever uses that word, jam their email. Crash their servers. And get us their flight schedules.

KARL ROVE: We own the newspapers, the TV, the radio. What's left is the internet. Jam it. Crash it. Kill it. Call it Operation ChickenHawk.

PRESIDENT BUSH: There's two other words.

VICE PRESIDENT CHENEY: Right. Halliburton. And Harken. They turn up twice in any email, crash the damn computer. And get us their vitals.

SECRETARY RIDGE: Anything else?

KARL ROVE: Any TV or radio jock or print reporter who dumps on Halliburton or Harken, we bust them.. Look what we did to Howard Stern.

ATTORNEY-GENERAL ASHCROFT: Calling anyone from this Administration a ChickenHawk is an act of terrorism. Writing about Halliburton or Harken Energy is an act of terrorism.

VICE PRESIDENT CHENEY: Look at the ACLU. At Greenpeace. At the NAACP. The League of Women Voters.

ATTORNEY-GENERAL ASHCROFT: All terrorist fronts!!!

VICE PRESIDENT CHENEY: Exactly. This is a democracy. We don't have to stand for that stuff.

PRESIDENT BUSH: Americans have fought for the right to not hear about those things. That's why I joined the National Guard and learned how to fly.

SECRETARY RIDGE: But what if some of these transcripts leak out. Look at what happened to Nixon.

KARL ROVE: Back then there was an actual Democratic Party. Today we own the Democratic Leadership Council, the courts, the media….

VICE PRESIDENT CHENEY: Plus that goddam Bill of Rights. All gone now.

KARL ROVE: That's why we're taping these Oval Office conversations and putting them out on the internet. Nobody will believe them. And then we can do whatever we want and get away with it.

ATTORNEY-GENERAL ASHCROFT: Praise the Lord!

PRESIDENT BUSH: Hey guys, how's this: *L'etat, c'est moi*. Pretty cool, huh. It's a good thing I can speak Spanish!!

THREE: DECEMBER, 2003
"All those liberals soiling themselves"

PRESIDENT BUSH: Well, are we going to attack Iraq, or aren't we?

KARL ROVE: We need to take it a little slow, George. Except for Tony…

PRESIDENT BUSH: Tony the Tiger?

VICE PRESIDENT CHENEY: Tony the Lapdog.

KARL ROVE: Tony Blair. Except for Tony Blair, the Europeans don't believe the Weapons of Mass Destruction stuff. They don't believe Saddam worked with Osama. They'll vote against us in the UN.

PRESIDENT BUSH: That goddam towelhead tried to kill my daddy.

KARL ROVE: Yes, George. And we need that oil.

VICE PRESIDENT CHENEY: Gas prices gotta come down, boys. We need the gallon under $1.50 by election day. That means one thing.

SECRETARY RUMSFELD: Kill the sonofabitch.

PRESIDENT BUSH: You kissed Saddam, Don. I've seen the pictures.

SECRETARY RUMSFELD: Reagan made me, dammit. We wanted him to gas the Iranians. And he did. Tons of em. Kurds too.

ATTORNEY-GENERAL ASHCROFT: Thousands of heathen Muslims gone to the Lord. Praise Jesus!!

VICE PRESIDENT CHENEY: Hell, if he'd gas a few choice Democrats, I'd kiss him too.

KARL ROVE: He's not your type, Dick.

SECRETARY RUMSFELD: Yes he is. Believe me, Karl, Saddam Hussein and Dick Cheney are birds of a feather.

VICE PRESIDENT CHENEY: Right, but I'm OUR bird and Saddam was our bird, too, and then he wasn't, so we now kill the sonofabitch.

SECRETARY RIDGE: God help the innocent Iraqis that happen to be in the way.

SECRETARY POWELL: And our troops.

SECRETARY RIDGE: Aside from trying to kill George's daddy, Saddam's chief crime seems to have been contemplating switching his oil transactions from the dollar to the euro.

KARL ROVE: You damn well betcha, Tom. Our whole economy is being propped up by the fact that the dollar is still based on those oil reserves. Saddam was about to undermine all that, which would have sent us right down the tubes.

ATTORNEY-GENERAL ASHCROFT: Switching the oil trade from the dollar to the euro is an act of terrorism.

VICE PRESIDENT CHENEY: Hitting the World Trade Center was a love tap compared to moving oil off the dollar. So we kill that asshole before he gets the chance.

PRESIDENT BUSH: We've got the Weapons of Mass Destruction thing and the Al Queda link. What the hell are we waiting for?

KARL ROVE: Well, there are no WMDs and there's no link between Saddam and Osama. They hate each other. Always did.

VICE PRESIDENT CHENEY: Colin, you go to the United Nations with this crap. That'll confuse the liberals for a while.

SECRETARY POWELL: Do you have documentation?

KARL ROVE: Confusing liberals is never much of a problem. They come pre-confused.

SECRETARY RIDGE: Some of them are not so confused about our killing Paul Wellstone. The internet's full of it.

VICE PRESIDENT CHENEY: Oh please, Tom, it's fringe stuff. Nobody's going to believe it.

SECRETARY RIDGE: They're still looking for the black box from Wellstone's plane.

PRESIDENT BUSH: So?

SECRETARY RIDGE: Well, sir, there's a discrepancy. We said his plane wasn't required to carry a black box. But there was one. So now we have to say there wasn't. But there was. And is.

VICE-PRESIDENT CHENEY: So trash the box and fix things with Ailes at Fox and Rush and our usual bloviators. Anybody that questions that plane going down, they're a kook. Pure and simple. Same with the Carnahan crash in 2000.

ATTORNEY-GENERAL ASHCROFT: Investigating the death of Paul Wellstone is an act of terrorism.

SECRETARY RIDGE: Well, but none of it really adds up. The weather wasn't bad. The plane was top of the line. The pilots were top of the line. I listened to what the box had to say and it wasn't pretty. And there was an eye witness on the ground.

SECRETARY RUMSFELD: Why does that box still exist? Why is that witness still alive?

SECRETARY RIDGE: But it's a crime to destroy an FAA box like that.

ALL: *Loud, prolonged laughter.*

VICE-PRESIDENT CHENEY: Tom, you just haven't got the picture yet. There's a lot of rumbling out there about this and that, and especially now about whether or not we should attack Iraq. But WE decide what's a crime and what isn't. Under the USA Patriot and Homeland Security Acts, YOU can arrest and even have killed anybody you want. You can also decide who is a terrorist and who isn't. Now repeat after me: "Anybody who claims Paul Wellstone was murdered is a terrorist."

ATTORNEY-GENERAL ASHCROFT: Anybody who claims Paul Wellstone was murdered is a terrorist.

SECRETARY RIDGE: The internet is full of reports that you personally threatened Paul Wellstone before he died that if he didn't stop yapping about the attack on Iraq, there would be serious consequences.

VICE-PRESIDENT CHENEY: I always keep my word. Ha ha ha.

PRESIDENT BUSH: I bet he believes you now!

ATTORNEY-GENERAL ASHCROFT: Another non-believer come to Jesus!

PRESIDENT BUSH: All this reminds me of my love for Israel. It's Jews I can't stand.

KARL ROVE: At least liberal ones like Paul Wellstone.

ATTORNEY-GENERAL ASHCROFT: Can I also say that anyone who claims Mel Carnahan was murdered is a terrorist?

VICE PRESIDENT CHENEY: Knock yourself out. You can even throw in JFK, RFK, JFK Junior, Ron Brown, Mickey Leland, John Heinz and John Tower if you want.

ATTORNEY-GENERAL ASHCROFT: Well, it certainly does heighten one's respect for due process. I haven't laughed so hard fun since you chose Henry Kissinger to head the 9/11 Commission.

PRESIDENT BUSH: Yeah, speaking of Jews.

KARL ROVE: Dick I could hardly keep a straight face over that one. All those liberals, soiling themselves.

VICE-PRESIDENT CHENEY: Ha ha ha. Well, you know what I always say about having a sense of humor in this business.

KARL ROVE: I knew he'd never do it. I'm sure he'd've done a fine job not finding anything we didn't want found about Osama bin Laden. But the idea of a Senate screening panel auditing Henry's finances was enough to prompt a call to his heart specialist.

SECRETARY RIDGE: That was quite a call. We listened in.

VICE PRESIDENT CHENEY: Just to make sure we're all on message here: we will stonewall any serious investigation into the September 11 attacks. We all know why, don't we?

PRESIDENT BUSH: Why?

ALL: *Long, embarrassed silence.*

FOUR: CHRISTMAS, 2002
"It cost good money to cut the balls off the Democratic Party"

PRESIDENT BUSH: Merry Christmas, Gentlemen. How's our war coming?

KARL ROVE: We're getting there, George. The Weapons of Mass Destruction thing is selling pretty well. So's the Saddam-Osama connection. I think we can sneak it through.

VICE PRESIDENT CHENEY: Just goes to prove: you can't fool all of the people all of the time, but if you have enough money and power, who gives a shit.

SECRETARY RIDGE: Resistance to our attacking Iraq is virtually unanimous throughout Europe and the Third World, including China and India. The United Nations will never agree.

SECRETARY RUMSFELD: Fuck 'em. Let's nuke France. Cholesterol in their food will kill 'em all anyway.

ATTORNEY-GENERAL ASHCROFT: That reminds me of an old French hymn.

PRESIDENT BUSH: Not old enough, John. Tony and the Burlesque guy from Italy are with us, right? ….

KARL ROVE: That's Burlusconi, George.

PRESIDENT BUSH: Right. Sylvia.

VICE PRESIDENT CHENEY: Silvio. He's not in drag, George.

PRESIDENT BUSH: Whatever.

KARL ROVE: We also have Spain on our side. You could practice your Spanish.

PRESIDENT BUSH: Right. Yo, Saddam, *chinga su madre*.

ATTORNEY-GENERAL ASHCROFT: How fitting. A benediction. Praise Jesus.

SECRETARY RIDGE: Bob Dole turned us down on the 9/11 investigation.

PRESIDENT BUSH: First Henry almost has a heart attack. Now Bob overdoses on Viagra.

VICE PRESIDENT CHENEY: When he dies, they won't be able to close the casket. Ha ha ha.

SECRETARY RIDGE: According to our tapes from the Dole bedroom, the only thing that Viagra does is keep the Senator from rolling out of bed.

PRESIDENT BUSH: We don't want that damn commission poking around our ties to the Saudis. They don't need to know about our flying Osama's family out of the country.

VICE PRESIDENT CHENEY: Nobody knows, and nobody's gonna know.

SECRETARY RIDGE: On September 12, 13 and 14 we flew more than fifty members of the bin Laden family out of the United States.

KARL ROVE: No need for the FBI or CIA or anybody else questioning those people.

VICE PRESIDENT CHENEY: Out of sight, out of mind.

SECRETARY RIDGE: Those were the only planes flying in the United States on those days. It may be difficult to keep those flights secret indefinitely.

SECRETARY RUMSFELD: Who the hell cares. They're back in Saudi Arabia where they belong and they're all rich enough to keep their mouths shut.

KARL ROVE: If the story somehow breaks, Fox will trash it.

VICE PRESIDENT CHENEY: Can we get CBS and CNN bought by 2004? I don't like independent news organizations left hanging out there.

KARL ROVE: Independent is a relative term. We've got people inside, high up in each of those networks. Our people at the Carlyle group and elsewhere are buying up the movie chains and the video stores. What's left is a few magazines, talk shows and the internet.

PRESIDENT BUSH: Get it done, Karl. We don't want those Molly Ivinses and Michael Moore's coming back to haunt us. I had to deal with her in Austin. Do you realize she's taller than I am?

SECRETARY RUMSFELD: Smarter, too, George. That's the real problem.

PRESIDENT BUSH: Well fuck you too, Don.

KARL ROVE: We're working on shutting her up, George. The Bill of Rights has been with us 200 years. It'll take a second term to finally get rid of it.

ATTORNEY-GENERAL ASHCROFT: The Bill of Rights is the work of the Devil.

SECRETARY RUMSFELD: Free speech is something we can no longer afford. I never liked it in the first place.

PRESIDENT BUSH: How're we doing on getting Lieberman nominated?

KARL ROVE: We're pumping a ton of money into him. But he's going nowhere.

VICE PRESIDENT CHENEY: Lieberman's a loser. It's Terry McAuliffe and Frum and those other DLC pushers you gotta buy.

PRESIDENT BUSH: Just don't let Kerry slip through. He's too damn tall.

KARL ROVE: It costs good money to cut the balls off the Democratic Party.

SECRETARY RUMSFELD: Hell, Reagan did that a long time ago.

KARL ROVE: Whatever the case, we have Terry McAuliffe and the rest of the Democratic Leadership Council on our payroll. Ditto the Ohio Democratic Party.

SECRETARY RUMSFELD: Why don't we stop wasting good money and just call off the damn elections already.

VICE PRESIDENT CHENEY: That's Plan B, Don. Or maybe we should call it Plan D in your honor.

KARL ROVE: You're mistaking millions for billions here, Don. These Democrats come really cheap. A few million here, a few million there and the party of Roosevelt becomes the Party of Mush.

VICE PRESIDENT CHENEY: Look at what Clinton and the DLC have done for us. George's daddy here couldn't get NAFTA passed. But Clinton did.

PRESIDENT BUSH: Yeah, we had a lotta laughs about that at Kennebunkport.

VICE PRESIDENT CHENEY: Billions in our pocket, plus they pissed off labor. And for what? .

KARL ROVE: Right, then the Telecommunications Act. For nickels and dimes these fool Democrats turned over the whole media to our client corporations. Fox, Clear Channel, Disney. Makes my job a piece of cake. Old Joe Stalin never had it so good.

SECRETARY RUMSFELD: I still read this leftist shit on the internet. Why don't we just kill that damn thing already.

VICE PRESIDENT CHENEY: Too many corps depend on the internet now. But that's plan I. After 2004, when it's clear sailing, I kill the internet, or at least its use by people we don't like. Filters, tracking, jamming, viruses, trojans….my boys at Halliburton have it all worked out.

PRESIDENT BUSH: That ChickenHawk thing. Don't forget that ChickenHawk thing.

KARL ROVE: Right, and Harken, and Halliburton.

ATTORNEY-GENERAL ASHCROFT: Using the internet to accuse the administration of being ChickenHawks is an act of terrorism. Investigating Harken and Halliburton is an act of terrorism.

SECRETARY RUMSFELD: I gotta say, getting the Ds to cave on Iraq just before the mid-term elections was a masterpiece. One minute they're yelling and screaming, the next they're giving us a blank check. How much did that cost?

KARL ROVE: Nothing. Those wimp Democrats will always cave on war. Daschle, Gephardt, Kerry, Biden, it's almost embarrassing.

VICE PRESIDENT CHENEY: Right. They gotta prove they're manly enough to go to war. They piss off their liberal base and get nothing in return.

PRESIDENT BUSH: They gave us a blank check to go after Saddam. So when do we go?

SECRETARY RUMSFELD: Tomorrow, godammit. What're we waiting for?

KARL ROVE: Love to, Don. But we need to make some kind of show for international support. Colin will trot up to the UN. We'll let the Europeans fart around for a while. We'll let the Democrats twist in the wind. Then we'll attack.

PRESIDENT BUSH: That sonofabitch tried to kill my daddy.

KARL ROVE: Right George. He's also going to get us a second term.

VICE PRESIDENT CHENEY: Plan D is we cancel the election. Plan A is we crush Iraq and they dance in the street. That makes you a hero, George.

KARL ROVE: Right, we take Iraq, drive gas prices down for 2004 and glide in to power. REAL power. PERMANENT power.

ATTORNEY GENERAL ASHCROFT: The Kingdom of Jesus is upon us!!!

SECRETARY RUMSFELD: I can crush Iraq. Just give me ten good men.

VICE PRESIDENT CHENEY: You'll have all the high-tech hardware you need. When you kill Saddam, they'll throw flowers at your feet.

KARL ROVE: Just do it quick, Don. We can't afford a long war. There's already the makings of a real grassroots anti-war movement out there. You've gotta get in, get Saddam, get the oil, get those bases established, and cut the troop deployments.

VICE PRESIDENT CHENEY: We're going to slip the Guard and Reserve in and out before anybody notices.

ATTORNEY-GENERAL ASHCROFT: Opposition to our war on Babylon is an act of terrorism.

PRESIDENT BUSH: Babylon is in Revelations. Armageddon. The Apocalypse. Billy Graham told me all about that.

ATTORNEY GENERAL ASHCROFT: The End of Days is upon us.

PRESIDENT BUSH: Right, John. Merry Christmas. But don't sing.

FIVE: NEW YEAR'S DAY, 2003
"It's right here in Revelations"

PRESIDENT BUSH: Happy New Year, gentlemen. You all hung over?

ATTORNEY-GENERAL ASHCROFT: We had some lovely fruit punch at our church social last night. I learned some wonderful new songs, too.

PRESIDENT BUSH: I'm sure you did, John. Let's hear em when we're re-elected.

SECRETARY POWELL: Reporting for duty, sir.

KARL ROVE: Colin, glad you could make it.

VICE PRESIDENT CHENEY: All set for your trip to the United Nations?

PRESIDENT BUSH: Why haven't we found those Weapons of Mass Destruction yet, Colin? What's the hold-up?

SECRETARY POWELL: They're not in Iraq, sir. They're in North Korea.

VICE PRESIDENT CHENEY: We've been through this before, Colin. We know Saddam isn't stupid. And we're not going to attack Korea.

SECRETARY RUMSFELD: Why the hell not?

KARL ROVE: A hundred million Chinese ready to swoop down on us again, Don. How will that play in Peoria?

VICE PRESIDENT CHENEY: The Chinese did it in 1950 and they've made it clear they'll do it again.

PRESIDENT BUSH: 1950? Isn't that when the Koreans attacked Pearl Harbor?

SECRETARY POWELL: Through Henry Kissinger the Chinese have made it quite clear they won't stand for us attacking North Korea.

PRESIDENT BUSH: That Dim Sun guy's a pigmy. He reminds me of Spud Webb.

KARL ROVE: We've been planning this attack on Iraq since the last attack on Iraq. The neo-cons drew up the plans in the 1990s. We have no parallel plans to attack Korea.

SECRETARY RUMSFELD: Plans? Who needs plans?

VICE PRESIDENT CHENEY: Korea has no oil.

SECRETARY POWELL: Korea has nuclear weapons, Saddam Hussein doesn't. Saddam Hussein has oil, Korea doesn't. So who do we attack?

ALL: *Prolonged Silence.*

PRESIDENT BUSH: OK, but Saddam tried to kill my daddy. And there is no mention of Korea in the Bible.

ATTORNEY-GENERAL ASHCROFT: And a great fire shall sweep down through Babylon, and all who accept Jesus will go to Heaven, and those who don't…

SECRETARY RUMSFELD: They're mightily fucked, right John? I say we attack Iraq AND Korea. Fuck em both.

SECRETARY POWELL: Henry Kissinger has suggested we arm the Japanese with nuclear weapons and let THEM attack Korea. He would like a fee for handling the arms sales.

KARL ROVE: Now THERE's an idea. We can finesse this whole thing through the Japanese. They haven't had an army since 1945.

SECRETARY RUMSFELD: That's when we nuked em. DAMN that was good!

PRESIDENT BUSH: Ike sure knew how to handle things. Maybe he should be in charge of the attack on Iraq.

SECRETARY RIDGE: General Eisenhower passed away quite a few years ago, sir.

PRESIDENT BUSH: Oh. I'm sorry to hear that. Was it sudden?

VICE PRESIDENT CHENEY: I don't think the Japanese have enough money for a new army. Or for nuclear weapons.

KARL ROVE: We loan it to them. We put these guys in power, we finance their weapons, which we sell them. We get them in debt. Then, every few years, we pick one, like Saddam, to hype up for attack.

VICE PRESIDENT CHENEY: Re-arming Japan would be a hell of a stimulus package for my pals at you-know-where.

PRESIDENT BUSH: How about Kenny-boy. He could use some business now, too. I wonder if he speaks Japanese.

SECRETARY POWELL: Re-arming Japan would completely destabilize East Asia. The Chinese would be livid. So would the Koreans, the Vietnamese, the Indonesians.

PRESIDENT BUSH: Those places aren't in the Bible. We are the City Upon the Hill. And I'm the most powerful man the world has ever seen.

SECRETARY POWELL: We lost a lot of good people in Korea. I think we learned some hard lessons there and in Vietnam about land wars in Asia.

PRESIDENT BUSH: I wasn't in either place. I don't care. All I know is, we will bomb Iraq. Soon.

SECRETARY RIDGE: We've been bombing Iraq for twelve years now, sir.

PRESIDENT BUSH: I mean we're going to invade. We're going to kill Saddam Hussein. We're going to get that oil. We're going to fulfill Biblical prophecy.

ATTORNEY-GENERAL ASHCROFT: Hallelujah!!

SECRETARY POWELL: With all due respects, sir, the public is well aware that we haven't found those Weapons of Mass Destruction.

VICE PRESIDENT CHENEY: We sold them to him, Colin. We've got the receipts.

SECRETARY POWELL: But they're…

KARL ROVE: Colin, we are here to serve the people who put us in office. A lot of them are short sellers who are counting on the market to tank, at least briefly, when the war hits.

VICE PRESIDENT CHENEY: We don't let our people down, Colin. Just like you didn't at My Lai.

SECRETARY POWELL: Our people?

KARL ROVE: Colin, in this past mid-term election, where we took definitive control of the United States government, we outspent the Democrats by $180 million. Where do you think that money came from?

VICE PRESIDENT CHENEY: And we must complement you on the job your son Michael is doing over at the Federal Communications Commission, Colin.

KARL ROVE: By the time he's finished, there won't be an independent radio or TV station left anywhere in America. And I do mean left.

SECRETARY POWELL: Well, thank you. Michael does what he can. Protecting a free, democratic media takes eternal vigilance.

ALL: *Loud, prolonged laughter.*

PRESIDENT BUSH: Colin, it's good to know, on a day like today, that you can still maintain a sense of humor.

ATTORNEY-GENERAL ASHCROFT: Praise be for a New Year. May we smite Saddam and welcome Armageddon.

PRESIDENT BUSH: Colin, let me just make this clear to you: we are not going to war with Korea. Korea is not Babylon. We have been anointed to usher in the promised age.

ATTORNEY-GENERAL ASHCROFT: Hallelujah!

PRESIDENT BUSH: It's right here in Revelations. I am the chosen vessel. I am here to rid the world of evil. Like I told Bob Woodward: I am going to export death and violence to the four corners of the earth in defense of this great nation, and to usher in the new age. And it's all going to start in Babylon. That's what the Bible says. That's why we will attack Iraq.

KARL ROVE: Happy New Year, everybody.

SIX: JANUARY, 2003
"They're all going to prison, Colin"

PRESIDENT BUSH: Alright, guys. What's the holdup? Why haven't we attacked yet?

KARL ROVE: George, you've got to be patient. We're trying to build support for this war. You remember what your father did when he did Desert Storm.

PRESIDENT BUSH: Right. He put together a coalition of the willing.

SECRETARY RIDGE: George H.W. Bush campaigned for months throughout the world to build broad support for the military operation which forced Saddam to retreat from Kuwait.

PRESIDENT BUSH: That's my daddy. Always the diplomat.

KARL ROVE: So we'd like to do something similar now.

VICE PRESIDENT CHENEY: I told George he should've killed Saddam when he had the chance.

SECRETARY POWELL: That's not what you said in public. In fact both you and George Bush Senior made it clear going into Baghdad would have been a horribly bloody, costly mistake.

SECRETARY RIDGE: Dick, both you and General Schwartzkopf, along with the first President Bush, were widely quoted as saying going into Baghdad would have cost too many lives and would have destabilized the region and would have caused more problems than it was worth.

PRESIDENT BUSH: Well now that the Saudis have kindly attacked us we don't have to worry about any of that.

SECRETARY POWELL: There is still no convincing evidence that Saddam Hussein was in any way linked to Al Quaeda or the attack on the World Trade Center.

KARL ROVE: It's your job to change that, Colin. The key word is "convincing." We can link Saddam to Osama. We can scrape up some Weapons of Mass Destruction. We need you to sell the package.

VICE PRESIDENT CHENEY: We have CIA documents clearly showing that Saddam is building nuclear weapons, and that he has close ties with Al Queda.

SECRETARY POWELL: I know all about those documents, Dick. You went over to the CIA day after day and beat hell out of those people until they gave you what you wanted.

VICE PRESIDENT CHENEY: What? My Lai? Ha ha ha.

KARL ROVE: You can't prove it, Colin. Nobody can. There's no paper trail. The people Dick talked to all know what will happen to them if they say what you just said.

SECRETARY POWELL: Sooner or later it will all come out. We're already seeing a very substantial anti-war movement rising up, just like Vietnam. The demonstrations are large and growing. The petition numbers are substantial. Even many of the churches are expressing anger.

PRESIDENT BUSH: No churches I care about.

SECRETARY RIDGE: Actually, sir, the church you belong to has come out against the war.

ATTORNEY-GENERAL ASHCROFT: Churches opposing the attack on Iraq are hotbeds of terrorism.

KARL ROVE: That's where our control of the media becomes so crucial, Colin, thanks to the wonderful work being done by your son at the Federal Communications Commission.

SECRETARY POWELL: Thank you, sir. Michael does his best.

VICE PRESIDENT CHENEY: We know we haven't sold this war to the American public. And certainly not to world opinion. So what?

SECRETARY RUMSFELD: Let em howl. Makes em crazy when we do what we do.

KARL ROVE: Are you reading about the opposition in the mainstream press? Do you see any TV coverage? If a million people march and it's not on television, did it really happen? Or are they non-events, like Dick's trips to the CIA?

ATTORNEY-GENERAL ASHCROFT: Marching against the attack on Iraq is an act of terrorism. Televising those marches is an act of terrorism.

VICE PRESIDENT CHENEY: Colin, you're here for a reason. We have documents that show Saddam has nuclear weapons. All you need to do is get in front of the United Nations and read them. You'll be doing your people proud.

SECRETARY POWELL: Those documents are phony as $3 bills.

PRESIDENT BUSH: Do you think if we started printing $3 bills, we could put my picture on them?

SECRETARY POWELL: Under the circumstances, George, it might seem appropriate.

SECRETARY RIDGE: A recent report from Ambassador Joseph Wilson has confirmed that stories about Saddam's alleged attempt to buy nuclear materials from Africa are false.

KARL ROVE: We'll deal with Joe Wilson in good time.

VICE PRESIDENT CHENEY: He's got a wife who's a CIA agent. Maybe she could use a little publicity.

SECRETARY RIDGE: Ambassador Wilson's wife is named Valerie Plame, a key CIA operative. Exposing her could threaten the lives and careers of scores of her fellow agents.

SECRETARY RUMSFELD: Well, we would never DREAM of doing anything like that.

ALL: *Loud, prolonged laughter.*

KARL ROVE: Ambassador Wilson needs to rethink some of his conclusions. Can you help him with that, Colin?

SECRETARY POWELL: If Ambassador Wilson says this African nuclear connection is bogus and I go in front of the United Nations with it, it'll come back to haunt us.

PRESIDENT BUSH: Later doesn't matter, Colin.

ATTORNEY-GENERAL ASHCROFT: Later is after Armageddon, when the world has been cleansed and humankind has come to Jesus.

VICE PRESIDENT CHENEY: Remember what you did to cover up that massacre at My Lai, Colin. That bought us valuable time to keep prosecuting that war.

SECRETARY POWELL: Which we eventually lost. Maybe if the truth had come out earlier some lives could've been saved.

ALL: *Loud, prolonged laughter.*

KARL ROVE: Look how far you've come, Colin. Look what we've done for you and your son.

VICE PRESIDENT CHENEY: And look at the larger agenda. The attack on Iraq is just the icing on the cake. We've taken the entire conservative agenda and thrown it all at those wimp liberals in one fell swoop.

SECRETARY RUMSFELD: They still don't know what hit them.

KARL ROVE: The environment, the judges, the tax cuts, Medicare, tort reform, civil rights, the schools, church and state separation, women's rights, civil rights, the Bill of Rights, the whole nine yards. We've got them dizzy and tied them in knots

PRESIDENT BUSH: It's like what they call in Spanish a blitzkrieg.

VICE PRESIDENT CHENEY: It's hilarious watching these liberals scurry around like spineless little mice. No mercy. No compromise. No let up. This Iraq attack will nail it for good.

PRESIDENT BUSH: Compassionate conservatism, Karl. Makes my heart bleed.

ALL: *Loud, prolonged laughter.*

KARL ROVE: But we need this war, Colin. It divided and diverted the Democrats in 2002 and it'll win us the White House in 2004. After that, you can have whatever your heart desires. All of us can.

VICE PRESIDENT CHENEY: "Support our troops." Has there ever been a better campaign slogan?

KARL ROVE: How about "Support Our Troops & President Bush."

SECRETARY RUMSFELD: We still had to knock off Wellstone to get control of the Senate. Who'll we do in 2004? How about you, Dick? How's that ticker?

SECRETARY POWELL: I'm still concerned. Let me read you a quote I recently found from Winston Churchill about the uncertainties of war:

"Never, never, never believe any war will be smooth or easy, or that anyone who embarks on the strange voyage can measure the tides and hurricanes he will encounter. The statesman who yields to war fever must realize that once the signal is given, he is no longer the master of policy, but the slave of unforeseeable and uncontrollable events."

PRESIDENT BUSH: What's your point?

SECRETARY POWELL: We must be very careful, sir. Once we begin a war, be it in Afghanistan or Korea or Iraq, we have no idea where it will end.

VICE PRESIDENT CHENEY: Yes we do. Once we attack Iraq, the terrorists will eventually hit here. It will take them some time. But sooner or later, they'll come after our airplanes, our freeways, our schools, our nuclear plants.

KARL ROVE: We figure that will be somewhere around September or October of 2004.

VICE PRESIDENT CHENEY: Then we lock up the people really responsible: the environmentalists, the civil liberties creeps, the do-gooders, the peaceniks. They're all going to prison, Colin. All we need is for the terrorism to start.

ATTORNEY-GENERAL ASHCROFT: Demonstrating for peace is an act of terrorism.

SECRETARY RIDGE: The camps are ready, sir. We've got a Guantanamo in every state. All we need is for you to start sending me the prisoners.

ATTORNEY-GENERAL ASHCROFT: Demanding a lawyer is an act of terrorism.

PRESIDENT BUSH: Colin, it's late. Let me clarify one thing. We are not going to attack Korea.

ATTORNEY-GENERAL ASHCROFT: Korea is not in the Bible.

SECRETARY POWELL: The Bible?

PRESIDENT BUSH: Colin, I am the most powerful man the world has ever seen. I have a mission and a responsibility. Iraq is Persia which was Babylon.

ATTORNEY-GENERAL ASHCROFT: Praise Be!

PRESIDENT BUSH: It wasn't clear to me before that so-called election in 2002. But it is now. We have been anointed to usher in the promised age.

ATTORNEY-GENERAL ASHCROFT: Tell him, George.

PRESIDENT BUSH: It's right here in Revelations. I am the chosen vessel. I am here to rid the world of Evil. I will export death and violence to the four corners of the Earth in defense of this great nation. And it's all going to start in Babylon, just like the Bible says. That's why we will attack Iraq.

KARL ROVE: That'll certainly sew up the fundamentalist vote.

PRESIDENT BUSH: Votes don't matter, Karl. Korea doesn't matter. The Democrats don't matter. The media don't matter. Even the oil doesn't matter. What matters, Boy Genius, is the Final Battle. Armageddon. And we are going to begin it. Soon.

ATTORNEY-GENERAL ASHCROFT: Hallelujah!

PRESIDENT BUSH: Damn. I could really use a drink.

SEVEN: February, 2003:
"Armageddon is overdue"

PRESIDENT BUSH: Let's get going, guys. I don't like what's going on.

VICE PRESIDENT CHENEY: Calm down, George. Things are under control.

PRESIDENT BUSH: Well, I don't think so. What's with the damn United Nations? China. France. Germany. They're standing in the way. Who do they think they are?

SECRETARY RUMSFELD: Why the hell do we care?

KARL ROVE: Don't worry, George. We've got answers for all of them.

PRESIDENT BUSH: I want a war. God tells me we have to have a war. The economy is tanking. Gas is going up. And Armageddon is overdue.

KARL ROVE: Unfortunately, Colin's speech at the UN didn't really do the trick. Polls here went up, of course. But worldwide, he laid an egg.

VICE PRESIDENT CHENEY: I love how not a single US talk show or TV commentator raised the slightest question about anything Colin said. And the polls fell right into place, even Oprah's.

KARL ROVE: We've got every one of those networks in our pocket now. Thanks to Michael at the FCC, we can crack down on any talk jock that gets out of line whenever we need to. This nonsense about diversity in the media is over. Every US broadcaster is owned by one of our corporations. We also control their ratings.

PRESIDENT BUSH: What about that Phil Donahue guy? He's questioning the invasion, isn't he. Why's his hair white?

KARL ROVE: Not for long. We've sabotaged his ratings. MSNBC will axe him when we say so.

SECRETARY RUMSFELD: That's what I love about Rush. Nasty sells. Then he says he's just a showman.

VICE PRESIDENT CHENEY: Sending Colin to the UN was brilliant. Confused the hell out of the liberals. Nobody overseas bought the nuke line. But it sure sold here.

KARL ROVE: Love that Fox Network.

PRESIDENT BUSH: Poppy would have brought the UN along. But he didn't crush Saddam like I will.

SECRETARY RUMSFELD: Don't need 'em. Don't want 'em.

SECRETARY RIDGE: We're starting to see some pretty big peace marches. We estimate that about 15 million people recently marched worldwide.

KARL ROVE: Yeah, the European media is full of it. But you don't see any coverage here, do you?

SECRETARY RIDGE: They had about 500,000 marchers here in DC, about 250,000 in San Francisco.

KARL ROVE: But the newspapers said 50,000 or less here and hardly ran a picture. Not even the New York Times. NPR devoted more time to the Queen's new pants.

ATTORNEY-GENERAL ASHCROFT: National Public Radio is a nest of terrorists.

KARL ROVE: You can go public with that, John. Arrest them all after 2004. But NPR is really a bunch of gutless wimps. Threaten 'em once, they cave.

VICE PRESIDENT CHENEY: I finally read Bob Woodward's book about George. What did you do, Karl, give him some deep throat?

ALL: *Loud, prolonged laughter.*

KARL ROVE: That was also a nice job you did at the astronauts' funeral, George. Your graveside manner has really improved.

SECRETARY RIDGE: There were, however, extensive warnings from inside NASA of potential technical problems with the shuttle Columbia that just blew up.

PRESIDENT BUSH: Showing me those tapes of President Reagan and the Challenger was really a good idea, Karl. I think we made those funerals a plus for us, just like Ronnie did. .

KARL ROVE: The original idea was to have the Challenger up in space while President Reagan gave the State of the Union. He was going to talk to the astronauts from the floor of Congress. But the damn thing blew up.

SECRETARY RIDGE: The weather in Florida was too cold for the launch. There were extensive warnings that O-ring problems could lead to an explosion. But the administration wanted the photo op to coincide with President Reagan's State of the Union address.

SECRETARY RUMSFELD: Expert testimony made it seem the administration killed the Challenger astronauts by pushing too hard for an early launch. They should've just killed those experts.

ATTORNEY-GENERAL ASHCROFT: Testifying that the recent Columbia explosion could have been averted is an act of terrorism.

KARL ROVE: The Challenger killings didn't hurt us. It might've been better if the Challenger hadn't exploded. Same with the Columbia. But when you control the media, these things can be turned into a plus.

VICE PRESIDENT CHENEY: The Challenger funeral was a masterpiece. Ronnie looked very stately and concerned. Shed some tears with the families.

KARL ROVE: Our pundits gushed over how presidential and compassionate Ron looked.

SECRETARY RUMSFELD: If Carter or Clinton had blown up the damn thing and killed seven astronauts, we would have crucified them.

ATTORNEY-GENERAL ASHCROFT: It would have been proof of the wrath of an angry God.

SECRETARY RUMSFELD: We knew another shuttle was bound to blow. Those space crates are like rickety old school buses. The Boeing boys have been holding them together with bailing twine for thirty years now.

VICE PRESIDENT CHENEY: Yeah, but it was hundred-dollar-an-inch twine. Ha ha ha.

SECRETARY RIDGE: The high likelihood of another fatal shuttle disaster has been well documented. If there are hearings, the administration could be charged with criminal negligence.

KARL ROVE: George did a great job of furrowing his brow and looking heart stricken.

VICE PRESIDENT CHENEY: We control Congress. We're about to invade Iraq. Nobody's going to remember another crashed shuttle, even if we did let it happen.

SECRETARY RIDGE: But now the experts say they sent letters to the President.

PRESIDENT BUSH: I never saw any letters about the shuttle blowing up.

VICE PRESIDENT CHENEY: It was Clinton's fault, George. Just like 9/11. Gotta put the blame where it belongs.

EIGHT: VALENTINE'S DAY, 2003
"Terrorism is the health of the state"

PRESIDENT BUSH: England is with us. Italy is with us. Spain is with us. It's time to attack.

KARL ROVE: Well, they're not really all that with us, George. Tony Blair will send troops. But Italy and Spain are along just for show. If we do this, we do it on our own.

PRESIDENT BUSH: It's not a question of if, Boy Genius. It's a question of when.

SECRETARY RUMSFELD: How about tomorrow, George. I'm ready.

SECRETARY POWELL: We have no real plans for what to do with Iraq after we conquer it.

VICE PRESIDENT CHENEY: They'll be dancing in the streets. They'll be throwing flowers at our feet. What is there to plan for?

SECRETARY POWELL: We have seen some disturbing predictions about possible residual resistance once we get rid of Saddam.

KARL ROVE: We need a quick war. In and out. No mess.

SECRETARY RUMSFELD: What a bunch of damn pansies. We'll be done so fast you'll miss it if you blink. What was Desert Storm, four days? Give me two. Slam Bam.

KARL ROVE: We need Saddam at a show trial or dead. We need gas down to a buck fifty by October, 2004.

SECRETARY RUMSFELD: Can do. Let's go.

SECRETARY RIDGE: We're reading that since we just blew up another space shuttle we can't be counted on to precision bomb Baghdad without inflicting major civilian casualties.

PRESIDENT BUSH: That sonofabitch tried to kill my daddy.

SECRETARY RUMSFELD: Since September 11, there ARE no civilians in Iraq. They're all enemy combatants.

ATTORNEY-GENERAL ASHCROFT: Claiming there will be civilian casualties in Iraq is an act of terrorism.

SECRETARY RIDGE: Most of the rest of the world is against this attack.

PRESIDENT BUSH: Do they vote here?

KARL ROVE: No, but it doesn't look good, us going in alone. We need some international cover and just Tony makes us a little thin.

PRESIDENT BUSH: I'm thin, godammit. I jog. I lift weights. I wear blue jeans. I am God's messenger.

ATTORNEY-GENERAL ASHCROFT: Amen. None of the naysayers will be saved when the Heavenly fire rains down on Babylon and the Final Battle begins.

KARL ROVE: Right, and we like George's folksy Texas accent, too.

ATTORNEY-GENERAL ASHCROFT: Except for the swearing, George. Must you use those words?

PRESIDENT BUSH: You stop the singing, John, I'll stop the swearing.

KARL ROVE: But we need the American public to believe they still live in a democracy. We need them to think we actually care about bringing democracy to Iraq.

ALL: *Loud, prolonged laughter.*

PRESIDENT BUSH: That's the problem with Iraq. Saddam is dictator and I'm not. I've got nothing against dictatorship, as long as I can be dictator.

SECRETARY RUMSFELD: Too much damn freedom over there. Too much damn freedom over here.

VICE PRESIDENT CHENEY: Ditto that. We're nearly set for 2004. The voting machines are almost all computerized. Diebold has given us the codes. There's no more exit polling. No paper ballots. No audit trail. We can win any election in any state with just a few keystrokes. Look at Florida 2000. Look at Georgia 2002. Ain't democracy grand. Ha ha ha.

SECRETARY RIDGE: But perhaps there should be more discretion. Is it wise for Senator Hagel to own part of the voting machine company that arranged his election and re-election? Is it wise for Warren O'Dell, owner of Diebold, to promise to deliver us Ohio in 2004?

SECRETARY RUMSFELD: Some of Hegel's numbers in those black and native American districts were downright hilarious.

KARL ROVE: That's Nebraska, guys. Do we care about Nebraska? Do you see the stories on any of the networks? Our control of the voting machines is about as well-known right now as the documents we have showing Saddam and Osama really hate each other.

VICE PRESIDENT CHENEY: It's too bad any of that got out at all.

KARL ROVE: Saddam's people have always hated Al Queda. One is secular, the other fundamentalist. That's why the Iraqis had no interest in 9/11. Just don't tell CBS.

VICE PRESIDENT CHENEY: As if they'd run the story. Ha ha ha.

SECRETARY RUMSFELD: To most Americans, those camel jockeys all look the same anyway. Buncha towelheads.

SECRETARY POWELL: The cultural and spiritual differences between mainstream Iraq and the Al Queda terrorist network run very deep. It's not surprising the Iraqis were not involved. Remind me again why we're attacking them.

KARL ROVE: We have the White House, Congress, the judiciary, the media, the corporations, the banks, the military. But we don't have enough oil and without lower gas prices by November 2004 we don't have a guarantee we can get the additional four years we need to nail this country down once and for all. So we're taking no chances.

VICE PRESIDENT CHENEY: War is the health of the state. Terrorism is the health of the state.

SECRETARY POWELL: What's that got to do with national security?

SECRETARY RUMSFELD: Do you want those damn Democrat pinko liberals getting another shot at the White House? You want another Bill Clinton in here, soiling the carpets?

KARL ROVE: We look strong in the polls right now, Colin. But remember what happened to Bush I. His popularity ratings were in the nineties. A year later, he was out. We can't take that chance. We need a war.

VICE PRESIDENT CHENEY: One we can win quick. And alone.

KARL ROVE: We need to give the impression we're looking for global support. Then we take out Saddam ourselves and we're the heroes.

VICE PRESIDENT BUSH: Did we burn George's National Guard records yet?

SECRETARY RIDGE: That's being taken care of, sir.

KARL ROVE: We can't afford a Democratic president to come in here and look at what we've been doing. We're laying the foundation for a thousand-year...er, a long Republican rule. Democracy has had its day.

ATTORNEY-GENERAL ASHCROFT: Advocating democracy is an act of terrorism.

KARL ROVE: So it's simple, Colin. You keep plugging away at the United Nations. Meanwhile John will jack up the death penalty.

PRESIDENT BUSH: Ooooh, the death penalty. I LOVE the death penalty.

KARL ROVE: Keep busting the medical marijuana people. Throw the enviros in prison.

ATTORNEY-GENERAL ASHCROFT: We're looking for new ways to crush Greenpeace. We have some imaginative prosecutions lined up.

KARL ROVE: Lock up the liberal commentators.

VICE PRESIDENT CHENEY: We did that already. Both of them. Ha ha ha.

KARL ROVE: Dust off the concentration camps. Scare the pants off those do-gooder creeps.

ATTORNEY-GENERAL ASHCROFT: The Bill of Rights is an act of terrorism. Free speech is an act of terrorism. States rights is an act of terrorism. Smoking marijuana is an act of terrorism.

SECRETARY POWELL: Sounds to me like we're trying to emulate the Nazis.

PRESIDENT BUSH: My grand-daddy Prescott made good money bankrolling the Nazis. They had some good ideas and they paid their bills right on time.

SECRETARY POWELL: Some of the European press is starting to compare Guantanamo to the concentration camps.

SECRETARY RUMSFELD: Ha!!! I was just there. To be in an eight-by-eight cell in beautiful, sunny Guantanamo By is not inhumane. It's more like a free vacation. We should be charging them.

VICE PRESIDENT CHENEY: We ARE charging them, Don. With electrical wire.

ALL: *Loud, prolonged laughter.*

PRESIDENT BUSH: Some people call that sort of thing torture. I call it physical therapy.

KARL ROVE: We need the usual suspects out there playing the Church card right now. Get Billy Graham back on the war path. Rev up Falwell and Robertson. Get Rush on the prayer circuit.

SECRETARY RIDGE: First you better get him off Oxyconten.

SECRETARY RUMSFELD: Getting him in a stable relationship might help, too. How many times he been married? Are we sure he's not gay?

ATTORNEY-GENERAL ASHCROFT: Revelations and Ezekiel are the only UN resolutions we need. That's our God-given oil and that's our Armageddon.

PRESIDENT BUSH: I am the anointed, chosen to bring down God's holy judgment, starting in Babylon. So screw the UN and lets attack already.

NINE: March, 2003
"Democracy is for wimps"

PRESIDENT BUSH: (Yelling) WHAT THE HELL IS GOING ON? Where is my war? I want my war!!!

VICE PRESIDENT CHENEY: Calm down, George. We've got some problems.

PRESIDENT BUSH: Problems? We have NO problems. We are prepared to attack. I say it's time to attack. Billy Graham says it's time to attack. God says it's time to attack.

ATTORNEY-GENERAL ASHCROFT: Armageddon won't wait.

KARL ROVE: Well, George, I'm afraid we're no longer on such firm ground. The latest polls here show very serious resistance to our attacking Iraq without UN approval.

SECRETARY RUMSFELD: We win quick, we win big, they'll all shut up.

PRESIDENT BUSH: The Democrats have already caved, for God's sake.

VICE PRESIDENT CHENEY: Well that's a given.

PRESIDENT BUSH: Screw those peace marches. We're not running this government by focus groups. We're not running this war by some damn hippie pinko Beatle types. George W. Bush is running it by the word of God as brought to earth by Billy Graham and the Reverend Sun Myung Moon.

ATTORNEY-GENERAL ASHCROFT: Amen, George. Amen.

SECRETARY POWELL: Saddam just blew up his missiles, as the UN asked him to. How does it make us look if we attack him now?

PRESIDENT BUSH: Potent as all hell.

VICE PRESIDENT CHENEY: How does it make the UN look if they got him to disarm and then we attack him. Bye bye arms control. Ha ha ha.

SECRETARY RUMSFELD: Good riddance, too.

KARL ROVE: The negative numbers are just too high. Tony Blair's about to get lynched.

SECRETARY RUMSFELD: We've got Bulgaria. We've got Turkey.

SECRETARY POWELL: Actually, we don't have Turkey. They're rioting in Istanbul. They're not sending troops.

SECRETARY RUMSFELD: Alright Colin. Alright Karl. You tell me. We've shipped 200,000 people over there. We've pulled firefighters and mail carriers and nurses and sales reps off their jobs and away from their families. We're shipping Coast Guard cutters over there. How the hell do we bring them home without a goddam war to justify our having sent them there in the first place?

PRESIDENT BUSH: We don't, dammit. We attack already!!

KARL ROVE: Give us just a little more time. We'll get you a war.

PRESIDENT BUSH: Time!! It's March!! It's getting hot over there. We attack or we come home, which means we attack.

ATTORNEY-GENERAL ASHCROFT: Why not ask the Pope to explain the word of God to the world so we can fulfill His prophecy?

KARL ROVE: We tried that. He's against us.

VICE PRESIDENT CHENEY: We offered him a ton of money. Some serious oil leases. But he's against our attack on Iraq. Doesn't like the death penalty either.

PRESIDENT BUSH: Jesus Christ! What kind of Christian is he?

KARL ROVE: He's old, George. He keeps rambling on about the sanctity of life.

SECRETARY POWELL: Imagine that!

PRESIDENT BUSH: I think it's time for a new Pope.

SECRETARY RIDGE: The Pope doesn't fly on small private planes, sir.

PRESIDENT BUSH: Yeah, I remember now: He wanted me to not fry that Karla Faye Tucker just because she came to Jesus. Remember how I did her for Tucker Carlson: "Ooooooh….save me….save me."

KARL ROVE: Not a great moment in television, George. Lets hope the Democrats don't get their hands on that footage. Mocking a Christian woman you're about to execute is not smart politics.

PRESIDENT BUSH: She's dead. Who cares. Are you on edge today, Turdblossom?

VICE PRESIDENT CHENEY: We're all on edge. There's a quarter-million Americans all hot outside Baghdad with nowhere to trot.

SECRETARY POWELL: Maybe we're about to step off a cliff. Maybe we have no evidence of Weapons of Mass Destruction, of an attempt to build a nuclear bomb, or of a connection with 9/11. Maybe choking on that pretzel was a Divine warning, George.

PRESIDENT BUSH: Well at least John here is still finding time and money to bust those pot heads. I hear you've got Cheech and Chong set for prison. Just what's needed to guarantee our national security.

SECRETARY RUMSFELD: Guantanamo would be perfect for both those hippie atheists.

SECRETARY POWELL: They've been there. They liked it.

ATTORNEY-GENERAL ASHCROFT: The best way to secure our borders and end terrorism is to abolish abortion and arrest all pot smokers.

SECRETARY RIDGE: Many pot smokers today are using it to ease the symptoms of AIDS and chemotherapy treatments.

SECRETARY RUMSFELD: Atheism. Free love. Peaceniks. Marijuana. These are the true threats to the American way of life.

VICE PRESIDENT CHENEY: Exactly. And what the hell business is it of those damn enviros if Ken Lay wrote our energy policy?

SECRETARY RIDGE: Dick, you know the Freedom of Information Act entitles them to find out.

ALL: *Loud, prolonged laughter.*

VICE PRESIDENT CHENEY: That's a good one, Tom. Like the Government Accounting Office suing me to get the information on Enron. All I had to do was threaten to cut their funding. Poof! No more lawsuit from the GAO.

SECRETARY RIDGE: There are those who believe Kenneth Lay will eventually be indicted.

PRESIDENT BUSH: Kenny-Boy? Indicted?.

KARL ROVE: We can't let it happen. He knows too much.

SECRETARY RUMSFELD: But he also knows what happens to people who talk too much.

VICE PRESIDENT CHENEY: Damn nice of him draft up that energy plan, though. Saved the taxpayers a nice bundle in steno fees.

KARL ROVE: That few billion in extra tax breaks for Enron and the nuke boys didn't matter, right Dick?

ALL: *Loud, prolonged laughter.*

SECRETARY POWELL: Seems to me we're a bit jaunty for being on the edge of war. A lot of good people are about to die.

PRESIDENT BUSH: Oh hell, Colin, lighten up. You're not scheduled to be one of them. At least not yet.

SECRETARY RUMSFELD: We better get off the stick. The Iranians are already starting to slip into the oil fields.

PRESIDENT BUSH: Well why doesn't Saddam gas them again. That's why my Daddy gave him the stuff in the first place. Isn't that why you hugged him, Don?

SECRETARY POWELL: He got rid of it. And we're about to attack him. I'm not sure Saddam's in the mood to do us more favors.

SECRETARY RUMSFELD: They're all salivating over there. The Turks. The Kurds. Iran. If we don't jump in soon all that oil is going bye bye.

PRESIDENT BUSH: This war isn't just about oil, Don. It's about the word of God. And me.

ATTORNEY-GENERAL ASHCROFT: Amen to that, George.

SECRETARY RUMSFELD: So we bomb at dawn, right?

TEN: March, 2003
"War is peace"

PRESIDENT BUSH: Still waiting, Don. Still waiting for the attack. Why? Why? Why?

SECRETARY RUMSFELD: We've got a line on Saddam's movements around Baghdad. We might be able to hit him from the air. Surprise attack. One fell swoop.

PRESIDENT BUSH: It's late, Don. I'm tired of waiting. Just blow off the doors and take the damn country.

SECRETARY POWELL: We have no exit strategy, sir.

PRESIDENT BUSH: Exit strategy?

SECRETARY POWELL: What happens after we conquer Iraq. How do we get out?

VICE PRESIDENT CHENEY: What makes you think we're going to leave?

SECRETARY RUMSFELD: You're not with the program yet, are you Colin?

KARL ROVE: We kill Saddam, we take Iraq, we crush the residual resistance, we establish a puppet government, we set up four very large bases from which we control the entire middle east, we begin pumping oil, gas prices drop, we win the election, we crush all opposition here and there. What's complicated about that?

SECRETARY POWELL: That's not what you've told the American people. That's not what I told the United Nations.

ALL: *Loud, prolonged laughter.*

SECRETARY RUMSFELD: Colin, why the hell would we fight a war to install democracy in Iraq when we're getting rid of it here?

PRESIDENT BUSH: I'm tired of hearing this war is about oil. It's about the will of God. And my role as leader of the free world, and my Daddy before me, who Saddam tried to kill, and then Daddy didn't get rid of him, but I will.

ATTORNEY-GENERAL ASHCROFT: Amen to that. Praise Jesus.

KARL ROVE: With all due respects, gentlemen, let's be perfectly clear what this is really about. It's about ridding our homeland of the leftists and hippie trash and the Democratic scum. Once and for all. We've gone to great lengths to purge this nation of the Bill of Rights and the other Constitutional roadblocks to clearing out the godless rubbish that infests this nation. We've put everything in place for high-profile disappearances that will scare the hell out of the general populace and make Chile under Pinochet seem like the Athens of Pericles. We can now arrest anybody we damn well please, anywhere, anytime, with no cause, no evidence, no warrant, no due process. We can hold them indefinitely, deny them media access, torture them, let them rant, do whatever the hell we want with any leftist lowlife we choose to pick up. We may or may not choose to continue the charade of national elections. But we count the votes and we can crush anyone foolish enough to cross us. This war is the icing on the cake, the final sealant. When we win it, when we control the Middle East and its oil, the Battle of Armageddon, as you say, will be over, and we will have won.

ATTORNEY-GENERAL ASHCROFT: Praise the Lord.

VICE PRESIDENT CHENEY: In case you missed it, Colin, part of the plan is to rub out a few of our alleged friends. I call it the Mobutu strategy.

SECRETARY POWELL: Does that have something to do with race, Dick?

VICE PRESIDENT CHENEY: Just prior to the Rumble in the Jungle between Ali and Foreman, our dictator in Zaire began clearing the air. He killed hundreds of his known opponents. No trial, no lockup, no publicity. Just shot em dead, left em in the streets. Very effective.

SECRETARY POWELL: That's well-known.

VICE PRESIDENT CHENEY: But he also rubbed out scores of his friends. Took a random sample of his most loyal followers and supporters. Shot em dead.

PRESIDENT BUSH: Ooooh. I like this.

VICE PRESIDENT CHENEY: He did it for the same reason we bombed Nagasaki. Because he could. Kept the edge on. Made em ALL nervous. Showed a willingness not only to use power, but to use it irrationally and unpredictably. Scared the shit out of everybody.

SECRETARY RUMSFELD: What's that tell you Colin.

SECRETARY POWELL: It tells me the world is in very serious danger.

PRESIDENT BUSH: Lets arrest Jeb. I'm sick of him.

SECRETARY RIDGE: But sir, you owe him the election. He stole Florida for you....

PRESIDENT BUSH: Poppy made him do it. Jeb was gonna let me twist in the wind. He wanted to run against Gore in 2004. But dad called him. I had to promise to keep his daughter out of jail. You're still on that, aren't you John.

ATTORNEY-GENERAL ASHCROFT: I am, George. But there's only so much we can do. We have laws in this country.

ALL: *Loud, prolonged laughter.*

VICE PRESIDENT CHENEY: We need Saddam dead. He knows too much. He knows who sold him those Weapons of Mass Destruction before he so conveniently disposed of them. He knows who gave him the gas to slaughter the Kurds and Iranians.

KARL ROVE: We've got Saddam penciled in for the summer of 2004. Then we nab Osama in October. Right around the anniversary of when your Daddy killed the deal that would have let the hostages out of Iran back in 1980.

SECRETARY RUMSFELD: The timing on that was perfect. The October Surprise. Made Carter look like a fool.

VICE PRESIDENT CHENEY: That's how Ronnie got in the White House in the first place. Bill Casey and George's Dad strung out the hostage deal, tipped the election. That's why we've got to string out this Iraqi war. We've got about 18 months to kill before we reel in Osama.

KARL ROVE: Nixon and Agnew looked into canceling the 1972 election. Turned out McGovern was so lame they didn't have to. If the Democrats choose somebody like Lieberman or Gephardt, we don't have to worry either. But if things aren't going our way next year, we may have to do what Dick would have done, which is cancel the election.

SECRETARY POWELL: The American people will never stand for it.

PRESIDENT BUSH: Don't misoverestimate the American public, Colin. Turdblossom here can handle them just fine. We're in the White House, aren't we?

KARL ROVE: Things are going to change very quickly now. Bombs will go off. In key places. With or without the UN, once we obliterate Iraq the media will cream themselves with war fever. Once they taste blood, anybody that speaks out is going down. Rich or poor, Hollywood celebrity or big-time labor leader, they're all going straight to the camps. No more marches. No more internet. No more liberal yap yapping. We win this war, our polls will shoot straight back up and we will shoot to kill.

VICE PRESIDENT CHENEY: We start with some really wild arrests. We call them Mobutus. We pick people off the street just for criticizing George. The bong dealers. That Ed Rosenthal who was raising pot for the city of Oakland. Greenpeace. The women. The blacks. Labor. The gays. Plus a few of our very good, high profile friends.

SECRETARY RUMSFELD: Bust em. Bust em all.

SECRETARY POWELL: But it all depends on you winning this war. What if you don't.

SECRETARY RUMSFELD: Doesn't compute, Colin. The war is won. Iraq is in the bag. And thus the United States.

KARL ROVE: What you don't get, Colin, is that there will be no let-up, no compromise, no slowing down. We want it all. We are all-out attacking the environment, abortion, minority rights, women's rights, the First Amendment, the Fourth Amendment, the Fifth Amendment, the Fourteenth Amendment, all international treaties, the necessity defense, drug laws, habeas corpus, the arts, the judiciary, Medicaid, Medicare, Social Security, the budget surplus, unemployment insurance, the voting machines, the states, the governors, the organic farmers, the medial marijuana people, the hemp growers, the sex educators, the school teachers, the trial lawyers, the shrinks, even the cops and the firefighters. Everybody, anything that shows the least liberal tendency, and even a few that don't, we will attack attack attack.

PRESIDENT BUSH: Wow. Cool.

KARL ROVE: This is for all the marbles, Colin. We can't let up, not even for a moment.

SECRETARY RUMSFELD: Are you with us, Colin. Or are you with Wellstone?

VICE PRESIDENT CHENEY: Look what we just did to that wimp Donahue. Now MSNBC is all war, all the time, just like Fox, CNN, CBS, ABC, NBC, you name it. You know the definition of a "liberal media," Colin. It's a station that has 100 patriots and one liberal. What the hell are they doing with that damn liberal?

ATTORNEY-GENERAL ASHCROFT: Allowing a single liberal to speak out is a sign of weak faith. It admits of doubt in the absolute righteousness of our cause.

KARL ROVE: The ultimate enemy is not dissent, Colin. It's doubt. Never doubt that we can do this. Never doubt we WILL do this.

ATTORNEY-GENERAL ASHCROFT: Never doubt that we are the anointed of God.

VICE PRESIDENT CHENEY: We are going to ruin those people. Every last one of them. Jail them, bankrupt them, ridicule them, isolate them, stomp on them, terrify them, break them, silence them.

SCRETARY RUMSFELD: Kill them!! Kill them!!

PRESIDENT BUSH: Jesus is here. He doesn't want any mess.

KARL ROVE: Democracy is for wimps, Colin. We can rig the voting machines. We can fix the polls. We run the media. We tell people how and when and what to think. But when push comes to shove, it's the very idea of elections that's the real problem. The idea of choice.

ATTORNEY-GENERAL ASHCROFT: If you let just one liberal on TV, people begin to think there are other realities. If you entertain the idea that someone other than the Righteous can have a voice, you admit to doubt, which is the enemy of pure godliness, which is us.

VICE PRESIDENT CHENEY: Saddam can destroy all the missiles he wants. The Security Council can veto all the resolutions we propose. But the first bombs dropping on Baghdad mark the end of American democracy and the birth of the New World Order.

ATTORNEY-GENERAL ASHCROFT: Ezekiel and Revelations, starting in Babylon.

PRESIDENT BUSH: Next time we meet, guys, we better be in Baghdad.

KARL ROVE: War is peace. Slavery is Freedom. Ignorance is Strength.

PART TWO: MISSION ACCOMPLISHED

ELEVEN: April, 2003
"We have brought democracy to Iraq"

PRESIDENT BUSH (shouting): ALRIGHT! ALRIGHT!! ALRIGHT!!! Saddam Fucking Hussein…down the drain!!!

SECRETARY RUMSFELD: We have conquered Iraq. Baghdad is in ruins.

VICE PRESIDENT CHENEY: Yessir! Yessir!! Yessir!!! It's all over but the Muslim call to prayer. How does that go again? Ha ha ha. .

PRESIDENT BUSH: That'll teach that towelheaded sonofabitch to mess with my Daddy. And that'll teach my Daddy that I…

KARL ROVE: Don't go there, George.

SECRETARY RUMSFELD: No more yapping from those peacenik creeps. No more stupid jerking around at the United Nations.

VICE PRESIDENT CHENEY: Oil prices plummeting. Fat rebuilding contracts all around. Fuck the GAO. Fuck the Democrats.

SECRETARY RUMSFELD: It's on to Teheran.

KARL ROVE: Democrats? What Democrats? Fox, MSNBC, Clear Channel, the networks, that's where the power is. All those gas bag lap dogs wrapping themselves in the flag. The whole American media, embedded right up my…

SECRETARY RUMSFELD: I loved Dan Rather groveling at our feet. What'd he say: I am at your service, o mighty Bush war machine?

VICE PRESIDENT CHENEY: Grovel grovel grovel. How we love our courageous, objective journalists. And that's the way it is, Dan. Ha ha ha.

PRESIDENT BUSH: Maybe we can embed Dan Rather down at Guantanamo for a while. I know a few other writers that can join him.

SECRETARY RIDGE: Ernest Hemingway often wrote from Cuba.

KARL ROVE: I love how the French and Germans are now yelping about all that big oil money pouring into our treasury.

SECRETARY RUMSFELD: The Republican Guard turned out to be a lot more Republican than Guard, didn't they boys.

ATTORNEY-GENERAL ASHCROFT: May I sing? (singing)
Onward Christian Sooo-oldiers, marching off to....

PRESIDENT BUSH: Ok Ok Ok John, we get the message. You're not the Dixie Chicks. We know that already.

KARL ROVE: And there are some things about John you don't know, George.

SECRETARY POWELL: Your celebrations might be a bit premature, gentlemen. The Republican Guard indeed dispersed, but we haven't recovered many of their weapons.

PRESIDENT BUSH: What about Saddam? Where's Saddam?

KARL ROVE: We held him back.

PRESIDENT BUSH: Held him back?

KARL ROVE: It's important to space these things out. We have a huge victory on our hands. The polls couldn't be any higher. But it's too early, yet. We're a year and a half out from the elections. Remember what happened to your dad.

PRESIDENT BUSH: Well, where is Saddam?

SECRETARY RUMSFELD: He's wandering around Iraq. On a leash.

PRESIDENT BUSH: Well bring him in, dammit. I want his head.

KARL ROVE: Not yet, George. We've got to time this out. Things are strong for us now. But we'll need a bump somewhere down the road, and that's when we'll bring him in. Maybe next summer. Osama too. Probably in the fall. It's not always going to be roses.

VICE PRESIDENT CHENEY: Like the ones they're throwing at our feet over there.

SECRETARY POWELL: Yeah, right Dick. We're seeing a lot more bricks and bombs from the common people of Iraq than we are smiles and flowers. It looks a lot like Vietnam to me. How thoroughly did you really think this out?

ATTORNEY-GENERAL ASHCROFT: Ungrateful heathens. Their time of Judgment is fast approaching.

SECRETARY RIDGE: Many Americans think our administration conspired with Saddam to arrange an easy conquest, which will prove an illusion. Many Muslims blame us for putting Saddam in power in the first place.

SECRETARY RUMSFELD: We put him in, we took him down, we'll bring him in.

PRESIDENT BUSH: You gonna kiss him again, Don.

SECRETARY RUMSFELD: The conspiracy nuts say he's hiding out at Kennebunkport. Any truth to that, George?

SECRETARY POWELL: A lot of things can happen now in Iraq, including prolonged guerilla resistance. I doubt this thing is over.

PRESIDENT BUSH: Take a pill. We are in control. Nothing's gonna stop us now.

SECRETARY POWELL: Stop us from what?

SECRETARY RUMSFELD: One problem. Saddam fell before we could plant anything that even vaguely resembles a weapon of mass destruction. We threw some aluminum piping around. There's a couple of shady looking factories. But that's about it.

KARL ROVE: We've got that covered, Don. Remember, Dick got the CIA to say that stuff was there. Push comes to shove, the CIA can take the heat. George Tenet can take the fall. He was Clinton's guy anyway.

SECRETARY RIDGE: The Vice President is good at covering his tracks. Look at the energy plan.

VICE PRESIDENT CHENEY: I figure it'll be about a year of screaming about the WMDs before there's anything serious to deal with. Are you sure we can't plant something in the meantime?

SECRETARY RUMSFELD: Pretty tough right now. The whole world is watching.

PRESIDENT BUSH: Where have I heard that before? Wasn't that a Beatles song? Before they got weird?

KARL ROVE: When the time comes, Tenet will go down. We've got Tony covered too.

PRESIDENT BUSH: Tony Scalia?

KARL ROVE: Tony Blair, George. He is Prime Minister of Great Britain. They sent troops to help us crush Saddam.

VICE PRESIDENT CHENEY: I'm sure Sy Hersh will be right on the case.

SECRETARY RIDGE: Seymour Hersh of the New Yorker Magazine is under our constant scrutiny.

VICE PRESIDENT CHENEY: You remember Sy Hersh, don't you Colin? What? My Lai? Ha ha ha.

PRESIDENT BUSH: I want Saddam. Now. This is a man who gassed his own people.

VICE PRESIDENT CHENEY: That would be the Kurds. They've already got their eyes on that oil. We may have to gas them again.

SECRETARY RUMSFELD: Hate to say it, guys. But we may miss Saddam some day. I know I do.

SECRETARY POWELL: Saddam Hussein was trained by the Central Intelligence Agency. He was a CIA hitman long before we put him in charge of Iraq.

SECRETARY RUMSFELD: He was a very solid asset for us. Why he went for the Euro is beyond me.

SECRETARY POWELL: I'm not sure those oil pipelines or refineries can be defended in the midst of a popular uprising. .

VICE PRESIDENT CHENEY: Get ready for months and months of those stupid leftists shouting their conspiracy theories.

SECRETARY RUMSFELD: I love it when they do that.

KARL ROVE: Just remember one thing, gentlemen. Whatever else happens, we have brought democracy to Iraq.

ALL: *Loud, prolonged laughter.*

TWELVE: MAY, 2003
"Mission accomplished"

PRESIDENT BUSH: Good morning, guys. I assume you all enjoyed the DVD I sent you of me landing on that flight deck.

KARL ROVE: Mission accomplished, George.

VICE PRESIDENT CHENEY: Gotta hand it to you, Boy Genius. That was one helluva PR scam.

SECRETARY RUMSFELD: Goddam media's licking our toes. Fox is wetting its pants.

PRESIDENT BUSH: I look pretty damn good in a flight suit, don't I guys.

SECRETARY RIDGE: Is that why you're wearing it now, Mr. President?

PRESIDENT BUSH: I wear it to honor President Lincoln. As you know, I landed on the USS Lincoln, and we did it that way to remind the country of how he stood up to the Koreans after they sank the Battleship Maine at Pearl Harbor.

VICE PRESIDENT CHENEY: Hell, George. It's great to see you making up for the time you lost back when we had other priorities.

SECRETARY POWELL: Yes, Mr. President. Best I can tell you spent more time during the Vietnam War getting your teeth cleaned than flying.

SECRETARY RUMSFELD: All potentially damaging records pertaining to George Bush's military service or lack thereof have been destroyed.

ATTORNEY-GENERAL ASHCROFT: Referring to the President's war records in public is an act of terrorism.

PRESIDENT BUSH: Hey, Colin. Lighten up. We just won a war. We crushed a dictator. We brought democracy where there was none before.

SECRETARY POWELL: That remains to be seen. What we did do is lie to the world about Weapons of Mass Destruction and September 11.

VICE PRESIDENT CHENEY: The CIA gave us false information. It's all their fault.

KARL ROVE: Relax, Colin. The CIA is programmed to take the fall. We don't expect a problem. But should one arise, George Tenet now has a nice Swiss bank account to fall back on when he resigns in disgrace.

SECRETARY RUMSFELD: I wish to hell Saddam could've held out a few more days. I had some great spots for that Anthrax. Plus some nukes. The whole nine yards. We could've let the UN find it.

SECRETARY POWELL: This isn't Texas, Karl. You may have done in Ann Richards and all those Democrats down there. But there are a lot of very big loose ends.

KARL ROVE: Colin, no one underestimates the potential impact of the public learning that Saddam had no weapons of mass destruction and no connection to Al Queda. And it is a very long time until the 2004 election, so we have a lot of ground to cover. But never underestimate our power to persuade.

SECRETARY POWELL: Or to mislead.

VICE PRESIDENT CHENEY: This "Mission Accomplished" stunt will keep them occupied for months, Colin. Not one member of the major media has dared open his yap about the war since we did it.

KARL ROVE: Look what we just did to the Dixie Chicks. They open their yaps in London, we bust them off Clear Channel and every country station in America. You think anybody else is gonna have the balls to stand against us?

SECRETARY RUMSFELD: Grabbing Clear Channel was a master stroke. When are you gonna bust that Howard Stern creep?

SECRETARY RIDGE: Bruce Springsteen stood up for the Dixie Chicks on his web site. Their tour is drawing huge crowds.

SECRETARY RUMSFELD: Bruce Springsteen? He's Jewish, isn't he…probably a member of the American Civil Liberties Union.

ATTORNEY-GENERAL ROVE: Defending the Dixie Chicks is an act of terrorism.

PRESIDENT BUSH: I hung out with a bunch of Dixie chicks down in Alabama when I was in the Guard. Sure beat going to meetings.

KARL ROVE: Point is, Colin, who do you think is going to really report on the fact that Saddam had no weapons of mass destruction? Do you think Fox is going to do a special on it? Will Dan Rather stop waving his little flag long enough to do the leg work?

VICE PRESIDENT CHENEY: We can thank Bill Clinton and Al Gore for the Telecommunications Act of 1996 which gave our primary corporate contributors the opportunity to buy up all the major media in this country. Nobody owns a radio or TV station in America who doesn't report directly to us.

KARL ROVE: Every news show, every talk show, even PBS, they're all in my pocket. Embedded is an understatement. So you tell me, Colin, who's gonna stand against us?

SECRETARY POWELL: You don't own the European media. You don't own the internet. You don't own the United Nations.

ATTORNEY-GENERAL ASHCROFT: The United Nations is a satanic den of heathens. They are standing in the way of Armageddon.

SECRETARY RUMSFELD: Who let those people in the country?

SECRETARY POWELL: We thought we had My Lai contained. Now it's a stain that will never be removed.

PRESIDENT BUSH: Who remembers? Who cares? They're all dead now. What's My Lai, anyway?

VICE PRESIDENT CHENEY: You know, Lee Kuan Yew, who ran Singapore for us, used to open up the media and stage elections every few years just to see who would yell and scream. Then Lee would rig the elections and a lot of people would just turn up dead. Or not turn up at all. That's what we're going to do here. Plane crashes. Car accidents. Rare cancers. Household mishaps. All those peaceniks are on a fast track to visit Paul Wellstone.

SECRETARY RUMSFELD: If I was Seymour Hersh, I wouldn't be buying any green bananas.

ATTORNEY-GENERAL RUMSFELD: Seymour Hersh is a known terrorist. Investigative reporting is an act of terrorism.

KARL ROVE: Don't worry about whether those weapons of mass destruction turn up in Iraq, Colin. You know what I did to the Democratic Party in Texas. So you know what's going to happen here. We haven't got the prisons going yet. I don't think you want to find yourself in one when we do.

PRESIDENT BUSH: Are you with us, Colin, or are you with the terrorists?

SECRETARY POWELL: I serve at the pleasure of the President of the United States of America.

PRESIDENT BUSH: Great. Who do we attack next?

THIRTEEN: June, 2003
"There IS no rest of the world"

PRESIDENT BUSH: Good morning, gentlemen. Glad to be meeting again so quickly under such happy circumstances.

KARL ROVE: Things are indeed going well. Soon we will have no Democratic Party to bother us. The United States will soon look very much like Texas. Or maybe...

SECRETARY POWELL: Still wearing the flight suit, Mr. President.

PRESIDENT BUSH: You got a problem with that, Colin?

SECRETARY POWELL: The sacred American tradition dating back to George Washington is that the President of the United States eschews wearing military uniforms.

PRESIDENT BUSH: *Gesundheit*. That's Spanish for "what are you getting at?"

SECRETARY POWELL: Washington, Grant, Eisenhower...they were among history's greatest generals. But when they became President they never wore the uniform out of respect for the American commitment to civilian rule.

KARL ROVE: That's about to change.

VICE PRESIDENT CHENEY: Civilian rule is a luxury this nation can no longer afford.

SECRETARY POWELL: Your father was a war hero, Mr. President. He never wore the uniform in office. Likewise John Kennedy. And Teddy Roosevelt.

SECRETARY RIDGE: George Washington was offered a dictatorship. He turned it down.

PRESIDENT BUSH: George Washington was a wimp. I've said it before, I'll say it again: I've got nothing against dictatorship, as long as I can be dictator.

ATTORNEY-GENERAL ASHCROFT: God speaks through George W. Bush. He is the Lord's dictator.

PRESIDENT BUSH: Amen to that, John. But don't write a song about it, ok.

VICE PRESIDENT CHENEY: Or if you do, let somebody else sing it.

KARL ROVE: You don't think, now that we have power, that we are going to relinquish any of it, do you Colin? You get power, you keep it, you use it.

ATTORNEY-GENERAL ASHCROFT: That God's law.

SECRETARY POWELL: I'm not sure how George prancing around the White House in his flight suit enhances his public standing, especially since he never saw combat himself.

PRESIDENT BUSH: I've raised twins and I've seen combat, and I prefer combat.

SECRETARY POWELL: But you were never actually IN combat.

KARL ROVE: No, but he's SEEN combat. We've all SEEN combat, Colin.

PRESIDENT BUSH: I saw *Saving Private Ryan* last week. Don't you think John Wayne would've been better than Tom Hanks?

SECRETARY RIDGE: Perhaps if John Wayne were still alive he would have gotten the part, sir.

KARL ROVE: Point is, Colin, America is under attack. And we're going to make the most of it. It means George gets used to wearing a military uniform, because we ALL need to get used to it. After November 2004, it's all uniforms all the time.

VICE PRESIDENT CHENEY: Iran is next, Colin. That's our oil over there.

ATTORNEY-GENERAL ASHCROFT: There are millions of Muslims in Iran, as there are in Iraq. God demands we convert them to Christianity, just as the Jews must come to Jesus as the final battle begins, which it did when we attacked Iraq.

SECRETARY POWELL: You want to attack Iran? I'm not convinced we've got things settled in Iraq yet.

PRESIDENT BUSH: Mission accomplished! Mission Accomplished!!

SECRETARY RIDGE: There are 1.2 billion followers of Islam. They are not flocking to Christianity since we attacked Iraq. Some think now that Saddam is gone, the Sunni and Shi'ite will unite and a Holy War will begin.

ATTORNEY-GENERAL ASHCROFT: It's begun! It's begun!!

VICE PRESIDENT CHENEY: You've got to get your priorities straight, Colin. You're thinking about Iraq and Iran as war zones. And they are. But they are also something far more important.

SECRETARY POWELL: What's that?

VICE PRESIDENT CHENEY: Profit centers.

KARL ROVE: Halliburton, KKG, Bechtel, the telecommunications companies, the arms manufacturers, the food suppliers, the uniform companies….you should see the contributions pouring in, Colin. It's a thing of beauty. They're making a fortune over there. And it can only get better. For all of us.

SECRETARY RIDGE: Complaints are already surfacing that the Vice President's company, Halliburton, is profiting from the war.

VICE PRESIDENT CHENEY: Of course they are! What am I here for? Public service?

ALL: *Loud, prolonged laughter.*

SECRETARY RUMSFELD: That's our oil over there, Colin. Nobody's going to mess with it, least of all those damn Iraqis. They can keep Baghdad. They can keep all that sand. The oil is ours. The bases are ours. So is Iran.

ATTORNEY-GENERAL ASHCROFT: In addition to bombs, we should be sending them Bibles. They should know that Jesus is coming.

SECRETARY RUMSFELD: Actually, John, we're sending them something even better than Bibles. Depleted uranium.

PRESIDENT BUSH: Pleated uranium?

SECRETARY RIDGE: Depleted uranium. It vaporizes when it explodes. The world's most reliable agent of cancer.

SECRETARY POWELL: Better than Agent Orange? I don't think so.

VICE PRESIDENT CHENEY: We manufacture most of our anti-tank shells with depleted uranium. It's dense and hard. When it penetrates it pulverizes into fine dust which is highly radioactive.

SECRETARY RIDGE: When people breathe the dust or drink it in their water or eat it in their food, they're virtually certain to get cancer. Their children---if they can have any---are often birth-defected.

VICE PRESIDENT CHENEY: Using that stuff takes a big load off the nuke industry. It turns a waste product that's expensive to manage into a very profitable item. And it opens a whole new cancer treatment industry in Iraq, as well as among our own soldiers.

SECRETARY RUMSFELD: We're carpeting the region with uranium dust. It calls a rapid halt to the birth rate. You see enough kids born with six arms and three legs and you think twice about reproducing, even if you can, which gets increasingly unlikely.

ATTORNEY-GENERAL ASHCROFT: Iraqi's sterility rate is soaring. It's God's will.

SECRETARY RUMSFELD: The peaceniks are whining that Baghdad is now the most radioactive city since Hiroshima. Who the hell cares.

SECRETARY RIDGE: But our own soldiers have been harmed. We only took a thousand overt casualties in the first Gulf War, but now 220,000 of those vets are disabled. A lot of their maladies are probably radiation-related.

SECRETARY POWELL: Even if the fighting is over in Iraq, which I doubt, that means many thousands of American soldiers, men and women, will be harmed.

PRESIDENT BUSH: But then all those vets apply for medical benefits.

VICE PRESIDENT CHENEY: Hell, we just chopped $25 billion out of the veterans benefits budget. We'll cut more if we have to. Only the dumb and the poor get sucked into military service. It's a form of natural selection.

SECRETARY POWELL: Excuse me?

KARL ROVE: He didn't mean you, Colin.

SECRETARY RIDGE: We all had other priorities during Vietnam, Dick. But when veterans get angry, they can be quite effective politically. Remember Senator Kerry and that crew throwing their medals over the Pentagon fence. They had a big impact.

KARL ROVE: In case you missed it, Tom, we executed a Gulf War vet right before we attacked Iraq. We sent a very clear message.

SECRETARY RUMSFELD: One thing about Saddam, he sure knew how to use the death penalty. Damn, I miss that guy already.

ATTORNEY-GENERAL ASHCROFT: Applying for veterans' health benefits is an admission of terrorism.

VICE PRESIDENT CHENEY: Lets just award each vet an artifact from one of those Iraqi museums.

KARL ROVE: Gotta love that looting. Our polls showed that destroying the Iraqi sense of history would demoralize the entire region. It seems to be working. Wait 'til you see what we do to the Smithsonian next term.

VICE PRESIDENT CHENEY: Halliburton has found a nice secondary market for those artifacts. Amazing what the rabble will pay for the rubble. Ha ha ha.

ATTORNEY-GENERAL ASHCROFT: One of those museums had the knife Abraham used to circumcise himself.

SECRETARY RUMSFELD: Abraham circumcised himself?

ATTORNEY-GENERAL ASHCROFT: He was a hundred years old at the time.

SECRETARY RUMSFELD: John, if God ever tells me to do something like that, he better send Jack Daniels and a whole bunch of his friends to help out.

PRESIDENT BUSH: I was circumscribed when I was born. My mother made them do it.

VICE PRESIDENT CHENEY: I bet it hurt so much you couldn't walk for a year. Ha ha ha.

KARL ROVE: At least they didn't take your whole unit, George. Not like we did to Tony Blair.

ALL: *Loud, prolonged laughter.*

VICE PRESIDENT CHENEY: Colin, we divided Europe. We wrecked the United Nations. We conquered Iraq. Now we're letting the Iraqis tear themselves to shreds.

KARL ROVE: We've got the money, the media, the oil, the voting machines. Nothing…NOTHING…can stop us now.

SECRETARY POWELL: Stop us from going WHERE, Dick?

KARL ROVE: Our bloviators now demand we turn our attention to domestic issues. We will finish off the peaceniks. We'll shred the Bill of Rights. We'll bury regulation. We'll clean out the courts. We'll let those electronic machines re-elect us. And the money and the power will roll in.

ATTORNEY-GENERAL ASHCROFT: Yes, and Armageddon.

KARL ROVE: Right. One people One nation. One Bush.

SECRETARY POWELL: But the rest of the world, gentlemen. They're not too happy with us right now.

VICE PRESIDENT CHENEY: The rest of the world, Colin? There IS no rest of the world.

FOURTEEN: July, 2003
"I want my flight suit"

PRESIDENT BUSH: Good morning, gentlemen.

VICE PRESIDENT CHENEY: Hello, George.

SECRETARY POWELL: What happened, Mr. President? Lose the flight suit?

PRESIDENT BUSH: Being cleaned, Colin. You'll see it again soon enough. In honor of George Washington.

KARL ROVE: Gentlemen, we're here today to celebrate, not to bicker. It's seldom I'm moved to great emotion. But we've accomplished one of the great goals of right-thinking people in the last seven decades. We have finally and definitively abolished Social Security. And along with it, Medicare and Medicaid. I hope you all realize the magnitude of what we've accomplished.

VICE PRESIDENT CHENEY: Yes, Karl. A proud moment for all of us.

SECRETARY RUMSFELD: You go, Karl. That damn socialist Franklin D.---for Demented---Roosevelt is doing wheelies in his grave.

ATTORNEY-GENERAL ASHCROFT: A monumental act of social terrorism has been reversed. At last the American people can be freed from their retirement funds. And their medical coverage.

PRESIDENT BUSH: What does kicking Saddam's butt have to do with abolishing Social Security?

KARL ROVE: The tax cut, George. The Congress just passed the biggest tax cut in US history. We could never say so politically. But we just gutted the Social Security fund. There's no money left for any damn liberal social programs at all.

SECRETARY RUMSFELD: The welfare state has been drowned in Grover Norquist's bathtub. I bet he peed in it, too.

SECRETARY POWELL: Knowing Grover Norquist, I bet you're right.

VICE PRESIDENT CHENEY: The only people that seem to have noticed are the usual liberals. Krugman. Ivins. The Nation. They'll get theirs soon enough.

ATTORNEY-GENERAL ASHCROFT: Pointing out that Social Security has been gutted is an act of terrorism.

SECRETARY RIDGE: Soon many elderly people will be bankrupt and in the streets. They won't have food to eat and they won't have medical care. This could prove to be a security risk.

PRESIDENT BUSH: Hell, Tom, old people that haven't saved enough in this land of opportunity just aren't fit to live. Look at my mom and dad. They worked hard and saved their money. When they retire, they'll be just fine. Why can't everybody be like them?

VICE PRESIDENT CHENEY: There are three legitimate functions of government, and only three: fund our military, subsidize our corporate backers, and arrest our opposition. All else is socialism.

SECRETARY RIDGE: Aren't we also supposed to protect the country from terrorism.

ALL: *Loud, prolonged laughter.*

KARL ROVE: Terrorism is the health of the state, Tom. Without it our polls would still be in the toilet.

VICE PRESIDENT CHENEY: Never forget it took six plane crashes to get us where we are today: two that wiped out Mel Carnahan and Paul Wellstone, and the four on September 11. Carnahan and Wellstone could have killed this tax cut. And without September 11…

KARL ROVE: Same with Clarence Thomas. Remember, George, how your dad got him on the Supreme Court even though the nation was in an uproar. Then he put you in the White House.

VICE PRESIDENT CHENEY: What fun that was. First Lee Atwater stuck Dukakis with Willie Horton. Then we put Clarence on the Supreme Court. Ha ha ha.

KARL ROVE: Of course we should thank Al Gore and the rest of the wimp Senate Democrats that voted to put Clarence on the Court. Never underestimate the willingness of a liberal to cut his own throat.

SECRETARY RIDGE: So why keep Al From and Terry McAuliffe on our payroll?

SECRETARY RUMSFELD: Those guys would lick a latrine to look mainstream.

KARL ROVE: It's petty cash. The Democratic Leadership Council has been worth millions to us. They do the dirty work of ridding their party of anybody exciting or innovative. What more could we ask?

SECRETARY RIDGE: We have no money to protect our harbors, our airlines, our nuclear plants. I barely had enough for the plastic sheeting and duct tape here in the Oval Office.

PRESIDENT BUSH: No wonder it's so goddam hot. Feels like Crawford in here.

VICE PRESIDENT CHENEY: There's no money for schools either. Just like we want it.

KARL ROVE: No child left behind has gutted what's left of public education in this country. We've imposed hugely expensive testing demands and then forced the states to pay for them. And they're bankrupt! That's what I call fun.

VICE PRESIDENT CHENEY: Except for our specific uses, government is over. Democracy is over. The Bill of Rights is history. America belongs to US!

ATTORNEY-GENERAL ASHCROFT: The Elect of God are at last in power. Praise Jesus!

SECRETARY RUMSFELD: Watch your ticker there, Dick. We don't want you croaking at the helm. At least not yet.

KARL ROVE: Right. Remember what happened to Nelson Rockefeller.

PRESIDENT BUSH: Nelson Rockefeller?

VICE PRESIDENT CHENEY: He died in the saddle.

PRESIDENT BUSH: Nelson Rockefeller was a cowboy?

ATTORNEY-GENERAL ASHCROFT: No sir, he wasn't. But speaking of that, there is an Indian you might ask Jesus about. His name was Tecumseh.

PRESIDENT BUSH: Tecumseh?

ATTORNEY GENERAL ASHCROFT: His name keeps turning up on leftist web sites.

SECRETARY RIDGE: Tecumseh was Chief of the Ohio Shawnee. He was born under a shooting star south of what's now Columbus. He was a charismatic leader who spoke five languages and assembled a large coalition of tribes against the whites. But he was defeated by William Henry Harrison at Fallen Timbers. His body was never found.

KARL ROVE: But in 1840 Harrison ran for president as a war hero. It was a beautiful campaign.

SECRETARY RIDGE: Except he gave a three-hour speech at his inauguration. He caught pneumonia and died a month later. They called it "Tecumseh's Curse."

PRESIDENT BUSH: What's that got to do with me?

SECRETARY RIDGE: After Harrison, every president elected on the twentieth year has died in office. Lincoln in 1860, Garfield in 1880, McKinley in 1900, Harding in 1920, Roosevelt in 1940, Kennedy in 1960.

KARL ROVE: Reagan won in 1980 and was shot, but he didn't die.

VICE PRESIDENT CHENEY: By the end of Ronnie's second term, Nancy was running the country, astrologers and all.

SECRETARY RIDGE: Many believe it was actually Nancy Reagan who ended the Cold War.

SECRETARY POWELL: I believe that may be accurate. She has also gathered a following for stem cell research that can't be ignored.

PRESIDENT BUSH: What's all this got to do with me?

SECRETARY RIDGE: Well, sir, you were elected in 2000. That's a twentieth year. Some people think Tecumseh might be out to get you.

PRESIDENT BUSH: But he's dead. Isn't he?

ATTORNEY-GENERAL ASHCROFT: He's an agent of Satan.

KARL ROVE: We can't let things like this fester, George. I've seen this Tecumseh stuff on the web sites. It's a perception thing. We've got to stamp it out.

ATTORNEY-GENERAL ASHCROFT: All mention of Tecumseh is an act of terrorism.

PRESIDENT BUSH: This is creepy.

SECRETARY RUMSFELD: Just do a search and destroy on Tecumseh's name. Arrest anybody that talks about him or that curse.

KARL ROVE: Crash their web sites. Burn the text books. Delete the dictionaries.

SECRETARY RIDGE: There's a town in Michigan named Tecumseh.

SECRETARY RUMSFELD: Bomb it. We can hit Ann Arbor, too. By mistake.

PRESIDENT BUSH: I don't like this. It makes me feel creepy. Like when I sat on that toilet seat in Alabama. Where's my flight suit? I want my flight suit!

KARL ROVE: No need to panic, George. After all, you weren't REALLY elected in 2000.

PRESIDENT BUSH: That's right! Gore won by 500,000 votes!! That should count for something.

VICE PRESIDENT CHENEY: Tecumseh has been dead for two centuries. He can't hurt you any more than those black people Jeb expunged from the Florida voter rolls in 2000.

SECRETARY RUMSFELD: Maybe we can arrange for Gore to meet Tecumseh face-to-face. That might take the pressure off. Right George?

PRESIDENT BUSH: I like that, Don. If you do that, you can attack Iran. Tomorrow.

SECRETARY RUMSFELD: Good. Now can we take this damn plastic and duct tape off the windows. It feels like Baghdad in here.

FIFTEEN: August, 2003
"George will run as a Peace Candidate"

PRESIDENT BUSH: Lets go, gentlemen. We have a lot to cover this morning.

KARL ROVE: We are beginning to map out our strategies for the 2004 election. Our prospects look very good indeed.

SECRETARY RUMSFELD: I hope that involves our conquest of Iran. Now that Iraq has fallen into place, what are we waiting for?

SECRETARY POWELL: If you think Iraq has 'fallen into place' you're dreaming, Don. And if the GOP election effort is as badly planned as your undermanned campaign, I'm going over to the Democrats.

KARL ROVE: Oh, the Democrats are great planners? Did you happen to catch the Gore campaign in 2000?

VICE PRESIDENT CHENEY: The money we pump into the Democratic machine really paid off then. And it will pay off again next year. We've already got their nominee chosen.

SECRETARY POWELL: And who might that be?

KARL ROVE: Haven't you guessed? None other than Joe Lieberman.

ALL: *Loud, prolonged laughter.*

SECRETARY POWELL: They'll never go for it.

KARL ROVE: How do you think Gore chose him in 2000? Do you think Big Al was on drugs? Or were some of our friends whispering in his ear?

VICE PRESIDENT CHENEY: Cost us a pretty penny to get Joe Lieberman on the Gore ticket in 2000. *Oy vey.* Ha ha ha.

SECRETARY RUMSFELD: So when do we attack Iran?

SECRETARY POWELL: There are more than fifty million people in Iran. They are much more powerful than Iraq. Their government is not unpopular. We haven't been bombing them for twelve years. We haven't starved them with sanctions. We haven't sent in the UN to disarm them, and we all know THAT won't happen again.

SECRETARY RIDGE: We planned the attack on Iraq for many years, since the early 1990s. But final victory may be elusive.

SECRETARY POWELL: Long before September 11 you were ready to hit Iraq. Or you thought you were. It's a mess. And now you want to attack Iran?

PRESIDENT BUSH: Iran is part of the Axis of Evil.

KARL ROVE: The attack on Iran will come the day after the November, 2004 election. We will build a case that they were involved in September 11. We'll claim they have weapons of mass destruction. And we've already started the war planning.

SECRETARY RUMSFELD: And there's no goddam exit strategy there either, Colin. That's our oil. Afghanistan. Iraq. Iran. We take 'em. We keep 'em.

ATTORNEY-GENERAL ASHCROFT: The road to Armageddon goes only in one direction. It has started in Kabul. Then Babylon. Now Persia, and the Garden of Eden.

SECRETARY POWELL: And I assume you intend to explain all this to the American people in the coming campaign.

PRESIDENT BUSH: I am a war president. God wants me to be a war president.

KARL ROVE: We're working out the details. We will have a plan in place a year prior to the election. But we already know the basic theme.

VICE PRESIDENT CHENEY: Crush the infidels. Cheap oil. Profits for Halliburton.

KARL ROVE: Not exactly, Dick. George is going to run as a peace candidate.

ALL: *Loud, prolonged laughter.*

VICE PRESIDENT CHENEY: Like I always say, in this business, it's important to maintain a sense of humor.

KARL ROVE: We will be running in a great American tradition. In 1896 William McKinley ran saying he wouldn't go to war. He and Mark Hanna stole that election from William Jennings Bryan by buying a few hundred thousand votes. Then the Maine blew up in Havana Harbor and McKinley blamed the Spanish.

PRESIDENT BUSH: I thought the Koreans did it.

KARL ROVE: Of course, the Spanish didn't really blow up the Maine, it blew up from the inside. But nobody knew that at the time. And then we conquered Puerto Rico, Cuba and the Philippines.

SECRETARY RUMSFELD: At least we were smart enough to keep Puerto Rico. Why we gave back the other two is beyond me.

KARL ROVE: Then Woodrow Wilson ran in 1916 saying "he kept us out of war." A few months later, we were in World War I. The Germans had sunk the Lusitania. Wilson said it was unarmed and screamed holy murder. But he knew otherwise.

SECRETARY RIDGE: Deep sea divers recently discovered a huge cache of arms and ammunition in the Lusitania's sunken hull.

KARL ROVE: Then Roosevelt ran in 1940 saying we wouldn't get into World War II, and somehow Pearl Harbor happened.

SECRETARY RUMSFELD: Somehow? He arranged the whole damn thing.

SECRETARY RIDGE: There is considerable debate about Franklin Roosevelt's involvement in Japanese attack. Many think Winston Churchill set it up.

KARL ROVE: Then in 1964 Lyndon Johnson portrayed Barry Goldwater as a war monger and promptly got us into Vietnam.

VICE PRESIDENT CHENEY: Talk about a sense of humor. That Gulf of Tonkin stuff was a complete joke.

KARL ROVE: And now we've jumped into Iraq based on weapons of mass destruction and Saddam Hussein's connections to September 11.

SECRETARY POWELL: Both of which are...

VICE PRESIDENT CHENEY: Highly dubious? Is that what you want to say, Colin? Well, wait 'til you see what we come up with for the attack on Iran. But the point is, it doesn't matter.

SECRETARY RUMSFELD: We need the goddam oil. What more do you need to know?

ATTORNEY-GENERAL ASHCROFT: It's the road to Armageddon. We are already on it.

SECRETARY POWELL: Well, maybe you want to win in Iraq before you move onto another battlefield. I'm not convinced Afghanistan is all that secure, either.

SECRETARY RIDGE: The Vietnam quagmire destroyed Lyndon Johnson's presidency, and it destroyed him personally.

VICE PRESIDENT CHENEY: Lyndon's problem was he gave a shit. We don't.

PRESIDENT BUSH: I do what God and Karl tell me to do. Then I take a nap.

SECRETARY POWELL: We are in for some hard times here. Saddam had no weapons of mass destruction. He had no ties to Al Queda. And despite having proclaimed "Mission Accomplished," I see a desert quagmire with no way out.

SECRETARY RIDGE: Public anger is mounting over not having found any weapons of mass destruction.

PRESIDENT BUSH: They didn't find Tecumseh either. And now he's out to kill me.

KARL ROVE: Nobody will remember. Nobody will care. We have eighteen months to absorb casualties and whatever else they throw at us. There will be Congressional reports. Exposes. Scandals. Body bags. But we control the media in this country. There will be no follow-through on anything.

ATTORNEY-GENERAL ASHCROFT: Four of every ten Americans accepts Jesus as their savior and George W. Bush as His messenger on earth. No matter how the liberals scream, our flock will vote with us. Praise the Lord.

SECRETARY RUMSFELD: And if they don't, we crush em, pure and simple.

KARL ROVE: Exactly right, Don. But let's talk about that later.

VICE PRESIDENT CHENEY: We can't break with tradition, Colin. We can't promise to bring peace and then actually bring it. No president ever does that.

KARL ROVE: Actually, there was one. Dwight Eisenhower. He ran in 1952 promising to go to Korea and end the war. And then he did.

PRESIDENT BUSH: Wow. I never realized Ike was such a wimp.

SIXTEEN: August, 2003:
"We kicked their butts in Vietnam"

PRESIDENT BUSH: Alright, get your asses in here. I've had about enough, dammit.

KARL ROVE: Calm down, George. You handled the press conference quite well. I see no real problems.

PRESIDENT BUSH: Turdblossom, these damn press conferences are a waste of my time. I could've been lifting weights or clearing brush. Why do I have to get in front of these atheist reporters and answer their questions. The great thing about being president is supposed to be that I don't have to listen to anybody.

SECRETARY RUMSFELD: Reporters were born to be shot.

VICE PRESIDENT CHENEY: Especially that Helen Thomas. Why can't we at least get her fired.

SECRETARY RIDGE: Helen Thomas has been part of the White House press corps for a half century. She's an institution. It would be politically difficult to get rid of her.

PRESIDENT BUSH: Then get her to stop asking questions I don't want to answer. That's not part of the job description.

VICE PRESIDENT CHENEY: There are many other reporters that can go interview Paul Wellstone. All we need do is call our pals who OWN the papers they write for.

SECRETARY RUMSFELD: They should have hung a lot of those reporters during Vietnam. We could've won.

SECRETARY POWELL: Won what?

PRESIDENT BUSH: Yeah, we kicked their butts in Vietnam. But the liberal media never told the real story. There was all this stuff about us losing, but never any coverage of what really happened, which I saw first hand in Alabama.

ATTORNEY-GENERAL ASHCROFT: The liberal media is a tool of Satan.

SECRETARY POWELL: Exactly whose butts did we kick in Vietnam?

KARL ROVE: George, we need you to do these press conferences from time to time. It gives the media a false sense of empowerment. It diverts their attention and makes them think we still live in a democracy.

ALL: *Loud, prolonged laughter.*

PRESIDENT BUSH: Why wasn't Rush here? At least he says what we tell him to say.

ATTORNEY-GENERAL ASHCROFT: Rush Limbaugh speaks for God.

KARL ROVE: We just got him set up at ESPN to do football commentary. We can't do any better than that.

SECRETARY POWELL: Oh. And have you heard what he's said about black people over the years? And do you know what percentage of the players in the National Football League are black? I'd say you set a bomb over there and then lit the fuse.

KARL ROVE: I'm sure whatever situation arises, Rush can handle it. And if he can't, we can.

VICE PRESIDENT CHENEY: I've fed him some humorous one-liners just to pep up his presentation. That should help. Ha ha ha.

SECRETARY POWELL: You mean like Rush calling the Ku Klux Klan a harmless social club famous for its family barbecues.

SECRETARY RIDGE: The KKK is on the list of organizations we monitor at Homeland Security.

KARL ROVE: Well, you can monitor them, but don't bust them. We have the computers rigged in Florida, and the voter rolls are again being duly purged throughout the former Confederacy. But when it comes voting time, it never hurts to be able to burn a cross or two.

VICE PRESIDENT CHENEY: Listen closely to what Rush says on the air. He's very subtle. He denies it, of course, but it's all about divide and conquer.

ATTORNEY-GENERAL ASHCROFT: Preaching racial harmony is an act of terrorism.

SECRETARY POWELL: So what am I doing here?

PRESIDENT BUSH: Why don't we add that wonderful Dennis Miller to the football games. He's so funny.

SECRETARY RUMSFELD: They tried that on Monday Night Football. The only good thing was we couldn't see his shit eating grin while the game was on.

KARL ROVE: Dennis was a nightmare. But we need somebody on football.

VICE PRESIDENT CHENEY: Dennis was unbearable. I had the mute button set to come on whenever he began to spiel.

PRESIDENT BUSH: We should get him his own show!

KARL ROVE: We did. He'll keep it until we don't need him any more.

VICE PRESIDENT CHENEY: I keep sending him material. Otherwise he wouldn't be funny at all. Ha ha ha.

KARL ROVE: By the way, Colin. Your son Michael is doing a heck of a job for us over at the Federal Communications Council.

SECRETARY POWELL: Well, that's one of the reasons I stay.

ATTORNEY-GENERAL ASHCROFT: Yes, it's excellent how Michael is wiping out the last vestiges of the liberal atheist media. He is indeed doing God's work.

KARL ROVE: The internet and a few independent outlets are the last barrier to our complete take-over of the American mind. We're writing the final chapter on effective dissent. We just need one more term.

ATTORNEY-GENERAL ASHCROFT: Toleration of dissent is a sign of weak faith. Any media that allow even a shred of liberal opinion to be heard has become by definition a part of the liberal media.

PRESIDENT BUSH: That's what I like about Rush. You can listen to him for hours and not get your ears polluted with a single phrase of leftist crap.

ATTORNEY-GENERAL ASHCROFT: Rush Limbaugh is Purified media. He does not fall into Satan's trap of allowing an ungodly point of view, even under the guise of debate.

SECRETARY RUMSFELD: You got that right. And John, I like how you've been erasing street protests.

ATTORNEY-GENERAL ASHCROFT: Thank you, Don. We are now rolling out the very latest in law enforcement. We call it pre-emptive detention. It's based on the same theory we used to justify attacking Iraq.

VICE PRESIDENT CHENEY: Right, now we say we attacked Iraq because Saddam was THINKING about making weapons of mass destruction. So now we can also arrest anyone who might be THINKING about going to a protest.

PRESIDENT BUSH: I can see into a man's soul through his eyes. That's how I knew we could trust Ken Lay. And Ahmed Chalabi.

ATTORNEY-GENERAL ASHCROFT: We are now arresting people who look like they are thinking of smoking marijuana. We can often tell by how they are dressed.

KARL ROVE: Detain them. Demoralize them. Declare them unfit and throw them in mental hospitals. Dick Nixon did it quite effectively in the 1960s and 1970s.

SECRETARY RUMSFELD: So did Joe Stalin. What a guy HE was!

VICE PRESIDENT CHENEY: I saw you arrested some jerk in Indianapolis who tried to wave the United Nations flag at one of George's pro-democracy rallies.

SECRETARY RUMSFELD: Why didn't you just shoot him?

PRESIDENT BUSH: I saw that flag. It was scary.

VICE PRESIDENT CHENEY: Thanks to the Florida model, the more people we convict of felonies the fewer dissident voters we have to worry about. And, of course, skin color is an excellent indicator of which potential voters we need to eliminate. As well as that look in the eyes I just mentioned.

KARL ROVE: It's all just mop-up now. Total mind control. No independent media. No educational system. No social programs. We are God. Who can stand up to us?

PRESIDENT BUSH: Tecumseh, dammit. I want him found. I want him destroyed.

SEVENTEEN: Late August, 2003
"Focused Democrats are known terrorists"

PRESIDENT BUSH: Not a good morning, gentlemen. Why are we catching so much shit about these weapons of mass destruction. Why does anybody care?

SECRETARY POWELL: Well, maybe because we used them as an excuse to start a war. Maybe because I got in front of the United Nations and told the whole world Saddam had them. And he didn't.

VICE PRESIDENT CHENEY: It's that bastard Seymour Hersh again, Colin. He broke the story of the My Lai massacre in Vietnam that you worked so hard to cover up. Now he's let the cat out about Saddam not trying to buy African uranium for nuclear weapons.

SECRETARY RUMSFELD: Why do we let people like that continue to live?

ATTORNEY-GENERAL ASHCROFT: Nosy reporters are known terrorists.

KARL ROVE: We called him that already. It didn't stick.

PRESIDENT BUSH: Didn't we get rid of the kid that wrote that *Fortunate Son* book about me? Faked a suicide or something. Has somebody suddenly developed a case of scruples here?

KARL ROVE: George, Sy Hersh is a little too high profile at the moment. And this story doesn't matter. We lied about Saddam's ties to Osama. We lied about the WMDs. We lied about the African uranium purchase. We outed Valerie Plame. We're now even saying Saddam wouldn't let UN weapons inspectors into Iraq when it was us that kicked them out. None of these stories matters. The media doesn't follow through. We have an unshakable fundamentalist forty percent of the electorate, control of the networks, the codes to the voting machines, the loyalty of the army. If we need to call in a terrorist attack, we can do that too. I am in total control.

VICE PRESIDENT CHENEY: Fart nugget on top!

KARL ROVE: That's Boy Genius to you, Dick.

PRESIDENT BUSH: Turdblossom. I like Turdblossom.

SECRETARY RUMSFELD: So can we stop sending the checks to the Democrats already? They're dumb as fence posts. Gripes my ass.

KARL ROVE: You miss the fun of watching these fool liberals wandering around, lost and confused. A few million bucks, a few ringers in their central office and they can't distinguish left from right.

VICE PRESIDENT CHENEY: They fell right in line with the Iraq attack because they're gutless and they thought a quick vote would clear the decks for the 2002 election. Next day two snipers start picking people off at DC gas stations and the embedded media can't talk about anything else. Who says we don't have a sense of humor. Ha ha ha.

ATTORNEY-GENERAL ASHCROFT: Focused Democrats are known terrorists.

SECRETARY RUMSFELD: Focused Democrats are non-existent.

SECRETARY RIDGE: Sometimes lies can come back to haunt you. Look at former President Nixon. Don't you think that sometimes it just might be better to tell the truth?

ALL: *Loud, prolonged laughter.*

VICE PRESIDENT CHENEY: Dick Nixon was too damn soft. He let guys like Magruder and Dean live. We won't make the same mistake.

KARL ROVE: Remember one thing gentlemen: no matter how bad things get over there in Iraq, we have triangulated responsibility for this attack to a bunch of Likudnik Jews. None of whom are in this room, of course. We have positioned Wolfowitz and Perle and Abrams and Podhoretz and the rest of those fool neocons to take the fall for the decision to go into Iraq, just like the CIA will take the fall for the phony nuke stories and the lack of WMDs.

VICE PRESIDENT CHENEY: We've also given the neocon community the impression we're prepared to stand by Israel.

ALL: *Loud, prolonged laughter.*

ATTORNEY-GENERAL ASHCROFT: All good Christians love Israel. It's the Jews that are the problem. They must come to Jesus or be annihilated. Or both.

KARL ROVE: And after November, if we're still taking heat for Iraq, we'll screw them both ways. We'll blame the neo-con Jews for dreaming up the war and the liberal Jews for opposing it.

ATTORNEY-GENERAL ASHCROFT: Either way, when Armageddon comes, they will be left behind.

VICE PRESIDENT CHENEY: *Oy vey.* Ha ha ha.

SECRETARY RUMSFELD: Anti-Semitism is the health of the state.

PRESIDENT BUSH: Prince Bandar has some Jewish friends. But they don't have any oil.

KARL ROVE: If Israel helps us keep gas prices down, we're with them. If not....

SECRETARY RUMSFELD: All the Jewish lobbyists in the world don't equal a ten cent drop in gas prices.

PRESIDENT BUSH: Some of those people think we actually like them.

VICE PRESIDENT CHENEY: Same with the Supreme Court. It was nice of Sandy O'Connor to help stop the Florida vote count and get us in power. But she's pretty shaky on some of these social issues, and that's an indicator of trouble to come.

ATTORNEY-GENERAL ASHCROFT: Pat Robertson has courageously asked the Lord to replace Supreme Court justices who go against His will.

SECRETARY POWELL: Since a vacancy generally opens on the Supreme Court when a Justice dies, how is that different from an Islamic death threat?

KARL ROVE: You mean a fatwa? I don't think Pat is about to kill anybody.

SECRETARY RIDGE: We are monitoring some his more extreme disciples. Their behavior is disturbing.

VICE PRESIDENT CHENEY: Let them be, Tom. What they do can't be traced to us. Believe me.

KARL ROVE: Sandy will go when we get our second term. I relish choosing her replacement.

SECRETARY RUMSFELD: And a few others that may be leaving very soon, though they don't know it now.

PRESIDENT BUSH: Tony Scalia will make a great Chief Justice. I think Judge Judy would also be good.

SECRETARY POWELL: Far from accomplishing our mission in Iraq, the death toll keeps mounting. We're going to lose thousands of our own people by the time this is done...IF it ever gets done.

PRESIDENT BUSH: We killed Saddam's sons and that still isn't enough. Blew em right away. We'll get Saddam when the time is right. But then what? What the hell do these people want? Blood?

KARL ROVE: Killing Saddam's sons got us one week media pass. It blacked out all the Americans that were killed that same time. It kept the focus off the economy. We got our money's worth.

SECRETARY RIDGE: The chief concern of the American people remains the economy. We do not seem to have an answer for joblessness and the decline in real income.

VICE PRESIDENT CHENEY: We need to remind people how bad things were under Clinton.

SECRETARY RIDGE: But...

KARL ROVE: Unemployment was rampant in the 1990s. There was poverty. There was corruption. There was hopelessness. Enron. WorldCom. Martha Stewart. 9/11. All Clinton's fault. Not until George was elected in a landslide did the unemployment rate start to drop and the stock market rebound.

SECRETARY RIDGE: But...

PRESIDENT BUSH: I remember that. And Hillary is responsible for gay marriages. And for all those priests molesting those little boys.

VICE PRESIDENT CHENEY: They even infected the world of sports. Rush has pointed out that Monica Lewinsky caused Kobe Bryant's sex problems. And OJ's.

ATTORNEY-GENERAL ASHCROFT: Oral sex is an act of terrorism. Sex is an act of terrorism.

KARL ROVE: Remember that a quarter-million Americans in Iraq are a quarter-million Americans with jobs. We can cook the employment statistics. But the war is a big help.

VICE PRESIDENT CHENEY: It sure has been good to me and Halliburton.

SECRETARY POWELL: What about the ones that come home dead?

KARL ROVE: They come off the unemployment rolls. And the welfare rolls.

SECRETARY RIDGE: The Muslims have declared a *mukawama shaabia*, a popular guerilla war, based at the grassroots. They say they will never stop until the Americans leave.

PRESIDENT BUSH: Bring it on. God has told me to act, and I won't back down, no matter how many casualties we take.

KARL ROVE: We can handle five, ten dead a week without much impact on the polls. No pictures of body bags or caskets. No official funerals.

VICE PRESIDENT CHENEY: The oil comes in, the military spending boosts the economy, our backers make huge profits, the media are amused. All the way to November, 2004. Then we show them what we're really made of.

ATTORNEY-GENERAL ASHCROFT: Blaming the bad economy on President Bush is an act of terrorism.

KARL ROVE: Martha Stewart can cover for Halliburton. We just have to time her indictments.

SECRETARY RUMSFELD: Martha Stewart raises funds for Democrats. She needs to be in jail.

KARL ROVE: She needs some media face time in handcuffs. Keeps the spotlight off Kenny Boy, right George?

PRESIDENT BUSH: Why not send her to one of those camps like I saw last month in Germany? My grand daddy Prescott helped finance those operations.

VICE PRESIDENT CHENEY: Very efficient. Great labor policies. Work makes people free.

KARL ROVE: Think Guantanamo, gentlemen. It's Spanish for Auschwitz.

EIGHTEEN: September, 2003
"Arnold's Three Commandments"

PRESIDENT BUSH: Alright! Alright!! Alright!!! Boy Genius strikes again. Arnold for Governor of California. I haven't had so much fun since I went AWOL. And believe me, that was a lot of fun.

VICE PRESIDENT CHENEY: Karl, you know what a great kidder I am. But I could never have dreamed up this one. Arnold Schwarzenegger at the helm of the nation's largest state.

SECRETARY RUMSFELD: Arnold is a one-man weapon of mass destruction. He reminds me of Saddam before he went haywire with the Euro. Damn, I miss that guy.

KARL ROVE: I realized long ago there was just one guy to dump Gray Davis. We couldn't run Arnold in the general election. That would mean debates and a long campaign and a lot of media scrutiny. To elect a specimen like Arnold, who is basically a circus strong man, you need, well, a circus. As when, for example, we run Mike Ditka for Senator in Illinois.

ALL: *Loud, prolonged laughter.*

VICE PRESIDENT CHENEY: Hell, Gray Davis is such a stiff he could be in a circus himself---holding up a tent. Ha ha ha.

PRESIDENT BUSH: Sometimes I get really moved by the opportunities we have in America. Where else could the simple son of a God-fearing, down-to-earth Nazi storm trooper become governor of our largest state?

VICE PRESIDENT CHENEY: Yes, and where else could an overseas colony like Iraq become such a juicy profit center for a humble mom-and-pop like Halliburton?

KARL ROVE: Here's what's really fun: Kenny-Boy and Enron gouged all that money out of California rate payers. And now the Democrats will lose. Ain't life grand?

SECRETARY RIDGE: Arnold's files include many extra-marital affairs and a few bouts with, shall we say, some men's problems.

SECRETARY RUMSFELD: He's married to a Kennedy. What do you expect?

ATTORNEY-GENERAL ASHCROFT: The Lord works in wondrous ways. Even a sinner has his place in God's plan. Hallelujah.

KARL ROVE: Arnold makes Clinton look undersexed. It's partly the steroids. And it's partly his compensating for being, shall we say, undersized in certain areas. So I've warned him to keep his pants zipped, at least for the duration of the campaign.

VICE PRESIDENT CHENEY: He better keep his shirt on too, Karl. Either that or get back in the weight room. Did you see that picture of him bare-chested in the Post? He looks more like Rodney Dangerfield than the Terminator.

PRESIDENT BUSH: Ooooh. How about Rodney for Lieutenant Governor. Is he a Republican?

KARL ROVE: Those are Arnold's three commandments: shirt on, pants zipped, lips shut.

ATTORNEY-GENERAL ASHCROFT: Inquiring into Governor-to-be Schwarzenegger's sex life is an act of terrorism.

SECRETARY RIDGE: But he's already being attacked by our church people. They say he's too moderate and that he's pro-choice and smokes marijuana. Some of them even say he's an environmentalist.

ATTORNEY-GENERAL ASHCROFT: God help us.

KARL ROVE: That's just how you have to be in California. We coordinated some right-wing attacks on Arnold just to make him appear more moderate.

VICE PRESIDENT CHENEY: Compassionate conservatism, Hollywood style. Ha ha ha.

KARL ROVE: There's a problem with his name, though. It pisses off black people twice. So from now on, we just call him Arnold. Got it?

SECRETARY POWELL: Fine.

ATTORNEY-GENERAL ASHCROFT: Referring to Governor Arnold as a Schwarzenegger is an act of terrorism.

VICE PRESIDENT CHENEY: This environmental stuff is out. We're selling Yosemite. Arnold can't stand in the way.

SECRETARY RUMSFELD: I thought we sold ALL the national parks, already. What's the damn hold-up?

PRESIDENT BUSH: We were hamstrung by Christie Whitman. She's history.

KARL ROVE: With Mike Leavitt at EPA and Gale Norton at Interior we can turn all the national parks into campaign cash. Those greenie-weenie Democrats had all that timber and grazing land and mineral resources locked up in public trust. Can you believe it?

SECRETARY RIDGE: The national park system actually started with Ulysses S. Grant, who established Yellowstone in 1868. He and Theodore Roosevelt, the great conservationist, were both Republicans. So was Richard Nixon, who established the basis of modern environmental regulation.

SECRETARY POWELL: I'm not sure any of them would like us trading public land for private campaign donations.

PRESIDENT BUSH: They're all dead. Fuck 'em.

ATTORNEY-GENERAL ASHCROFT: Jesus is coming soon, now that we have attacked Babylon. The natural planet must be scorched for his arrival.

PRESIDENT BUSH: God wants those parks sold. He wants that money in our war chest. He told me Himself.

SECRETARY RIDGE: Our attacks on the Ozone treaty on behalf of the campaign contributors who manufacture methyl bromide were not well received, sir.

SECRETARY RUMSFELD: I've been in those damn forests. If one of those big trees falls on a bunch of campers, five or six people could be killed. Trees are weapons of mass destruction.

KARL ROVE: Our environmental policy is simple: if you make a big enough campaign donation, you can do whatever you want to the environment.

ATTORNEY-GENERAL ASHCROFT: They must pay for the privilege of clearing the earth for Jesus to return.

VICE PRESIDENT CHENEY: As Ronnie Reagan said, if you've seen one tree, you've seen em all. Plus they cause pollution.

PRESIDENT BUSH: That's our environmental policy: "One tree left standing."

SECRETARY POWELL: Speaking of environmental policy, a lot of our troops in Iraq are extremely ill with some strange disease. Many are dying, as they did after the first Gulf War, and from Agent Orange. Many believe it's due to radiation from the enriched uranium in our anti-tank shells.

SECRETARY RIDGE: Half the soldiers who served in the first Gulf War are disabled in some way. The birth defect rate among their offspring has soared. So have childhood cancer rates in Iraq.

SECRETARY RUMSFELD: That's why we cut veterans' benefits. We can't afford them.

VICE PRESIDENT CHENEY: We also can't afford any more exposure on your connections to the Saudis, George. I hear that Michael Moore is making a film about it.

KARL ROVE: The Bush family has been doing business with the bin Laden family for decades. No movie by someone like Michael Moore is going to have any impact.

SECRETARY RIDGE: It's all over the internet. Soon it will be in some of the mainstream newspapers.

VICE PRESIDENT CHENEY: The oil is set to flow from Iraq. The profits will go where they belong: to Halliburton. Nothing else matters.

ATTORNEY-GENERAL ASHCROFT: Linking the Bush family to the Saudis is an act of terrorism.

KARL ROVE: Putting Arnold in charge of California will just about do it. Add that to Pataki in New York, Jeb in Florida and Goodhair in Texas and it's game over.

VICE PRESIDENT CHENEY: You bleed a hundred billion big ones out of a state, like Kenny-Boy did when he did electric deregulation, you open the door for an Arnold every time.

SECRETARY RUMSFELD: We did to California in 2000 what we did to Chile in 1973, not to mention El Salvador, the Philippines, Haiti, the Congo. You privatize, you blame the disaster on the liberals, you find a front man like Arnold, and you take over.

SECRETARY POWELL: These things can backfire. Look what happened to the Shah, Somoza, Suharto. You put these clowns in office they can blow back on you.

SECRETARY RIDGE: What if Islamic fundamentalists sweep back into Iraq as they did in Iran?

KARL ROVE: I don't know what will happen in Iraq and Iran. But I do know what will happen here. A few arrests. A few assassinations. Some well-timed terrorist attacks. Some Foxist media. The whole place is finished. It's over. It's ours.

VICE PRESIDENT CHENEY: That's what 2004 is all about. Closure. Finality. An end to American democracy.

PRESIDENT BUSH: Ooooh. This is so much fun. Afghanistan. Iraq. California. America. It's a trifecta, just like September 11. What's next?

KARL ROVE: What's left?

PART THREE: OSAMA IN OCTOBER

NINETEEN: January, 2004
"You've got to push the button!"

PRESIDENT BUSH: Arnold! Arnold!! Arnold!!! So great to finally have you here.

KARL ROVE: It's an honor, governor.

ATTORNEY-GENERAL ASHCROFT: Praise Jesus. You are with us at last.

VICE PRESIDENT CHENEY: Governor, I welcome you, Halliburton welcomes you, and, of course, Ken Lay sends his regards. He wants to remind you that had Enron not crashed the California economy....

GOVERNOR SCHWARZENEGGER: Oh, yah, I am well aware of what Enron did to my Democratic predecessor. We are grateful.

VICE PRESIDENT CHENEY: Gray Davis is pretty blue right now. Ha ha ha.

GOVERNOR SCHWARZENEGGER: You're not taping these meetings, are you?

SECRETARY RIDGE: No, no, of course not.

GOVERNOR SCHWARZENEGGER: So maybe you can tell me. What did Enron do with the $100 billion they took from California? Where did it all go?

KARL ROVE: Much is in our very well concealed offshore campaign accounts. It will be spent in an unexpected flood very near election day. You don't think we're going to let George Soros outspend us, do you?

ATTORNEY-GENERAL ASHCROFT: Arnold Schwarzenegger has come to deliver the Sodom and Gomorrah of California to the hands of the Lord.

GOVERNOR SCHWARZENEGGER: There are many girlie-men. This will change.

ATTORNEY-GENERAL ASHCROFT: It's times like these we should all kneel down and pray together. Can we hold hands?

GOVERNOR SCHWARZENEGGER: Kneel? Hold hands? Are you…?

ATTORNEY-GENERAL ASHCROFT: Well how about a song?

PRESIDENT BUSH: Oh Christ.

ATTORNEY-GENERAL ASHCROFT: Especially in your honor, Governor. It's an old German hymn: (singing) *Deutschland, Deutschland, Uber Alles…*

GOVERNOR SCHWARZENEGGER: WHAT!!! I HATE THAT SONG! I AM AUSTRIAN, NOT GERMAN!!

ATTORNEY-GENERAL ASHCROFT: But…but…your father….he was a….

GOVERNOR SCHWARZENEGGER: MY FATHER! WHAT'S MY FUCKING FATHER GOT TO DO WITH THIS!!!

KARL ROVE: Calm down, Arnold.

GOVERNOR SCHWARZENEGGER: ACHTUNG! SCHWEINHUNT.

SECRETARY RIDGE: Oh my God.

ATTORNEY-GENERAL ASHCROFT: No. Please….

GOVERNOR SCHWARZENEGGER: SHEISSKOPF!!!

PRESIDENT BUSH: Wow.

VICE PRESIDENT CHENEY: Unbelievable.

SECRETARY POWELL: Damned impressive.

ATTORNEY-GENERAL ASHCROFT: Yaaaaaargh....

Sound of shattering glass.

KARL ROVE: Uh oh, George. That was your mother's favorite coffee table. She'll be really pissed.

PRESIDENT BUSH: We'll just say John was drinking again. Is he ok?

ATTORNEY-GENERAL ASHCROFT: *Gurgle. Gurgle.*

GOVERNOR SCHWARZENEGGER: What a girlie-man.

PRESIDENT BUSH: That lift was mighty impressive, Arnold. He must weigh, what, 250? 275?

SECRETARY POWELL: And the toss. Very strong. Good distance. Gotta watch your back on those.

GOVERNOR SCHWARZENEGGER: Yah. I wrenched it once throwing Uncle Teddy in the pool. It depends on how you bend your knees.

PRESIDENT BUSH: Do you think you could do that to Michael Moore? I hear he's making a really nasty film about me.

GOVERNOR SCHWARZENEGGER: Oh yah, piece of cake.

KARL ROVE: How about that ice cream guy. Ben Cohen.

GOVERNOR SCHWARZENEGGER: No problem.

VICE PRESIDENT CHENEY: I threw somebody like that once at Halliburton. She paid us right away.

ATTORNEY GENERAL ASCHROFT: The light. I see the light.

KARL ROVE: He doesn't seem to be bleeding.

SECRETARY RUMSFELD: Ugh. I can't stand the sight of blood.

VICE PRESIDENT CHENEY: His head looks banged up.

SECRETARY RIDGE: It always looks like that, sir.

ATTORNEY GENERAL ASCHROFT: The Rapture!!! It's the Rapture!!!

SECRETARY POWELL: Probably more like the Rupture, John.

ATTORNEY-GENERAL ASHCROFT: The button, George. You've got to push the button. Begin the nuclear war. Bring us Armageddon. The Lord says it's time.

PRESIDENT BUSH: We talked about that, John. That's only if we lose in November.

KARL ROVE: Not gonna happen.

ATTORNEY-GENERAL ASHCROFT: Apocalypse! We need the Apocalypse. It's our charge to bring it on.

GOVERNOR SCHWARZENEGGER: That got me excited. Lets attack France.

PRESIDENT BUSH: Good idea.

ATTORNEY-GENERAL ASHCROFT: I was flying. I was flying.

VICE PRESIDENT CHENEY: Right, John. You're the flying nun.

ATTORNEY-GENERAL ASHCROFT: My God! You know?

KARL ROVE: We caught a glimpse of your undies as you traveled overhead.

ATTORNEY-GENERAL ASHCROFT: When I was...unconscious...I didn't sing that YMCA song again, did I? Oh, God..

GOVERNOR SCHWARZENEGGER: No, but you did name a bath house. It's in San Francisco. I know where it is. Many girlie-men there.

ATTORNEY-GENERAL ASHCROFT: Oh, God.

KARL ROVE: Don't worry, John. I've known all about it for a long, long time. It'll be our little secret.

VICE PRESIDENT CHENEY: Just keep busting who we tell you to bust.

SECRETARY RIDGE: Under John Ashcroft, there are 2.2 million Americans in prison. About 800,000 are there for victimless crimes, like pot. Many are cancer and AIDS patients who believe smoking it can help their appetite and general health.

SECRETARY POWELL: There is medical evidence to support that.

ATTORNEY-GENERAL ASHCROFT: Smoking marijuana is an act of terrorism. Contracting AIDS is a sign of Divine judgment. Criticizing Karl Rove is a capital offence.

KARL ROVE: That's right, John. How does that YMCA song go again?

```
TWENTY:  February, 2004
"Osama in October"
```

PRESIDENT BUSH: Alright, everybody. On your knees. We've been beat up these past few months. It's time to get right with the Big Guy.

ATTORNEY-GENERAL ASHCROFT: Dear Lord, we know you are testing us. We shall not be found wanting. It has been your will to make George W. Bush your spiritual vessel here on earth. You speak through him. He rules with your absolute mandate. Thus we can do anything. September 11 put this nation on notice that we can no longer allow it to live in sin or civil liberty. We have launched our holy crusade against the Islamics and their liberal minions. We have smote the Saddamites. We will imprison the Democrats. We have ignited the Holy Fire, as in Revelations. You have made this time of testing into a trap of illusions among those who would oppose us. Thanks to your grace, we will crush them at the first opportunity, especially after the November elections, if you wish us to allow them to happen.

VICE PRESIDENT CHENEY: Thank you for that, John. And thank you for not singing.

ATTORNEY-GENERAL ASHCROFT: I've learned my lesson.

PRESIDENT BUSH: I just want to add, Lord, that I appreciate you anointing me as your chosen saviorist here in America, and I will do everything in my power to prevaricate the mess we're in.

ALL: Amen.

GOVERNOR SCHWARZENEGGER: That was very moving, George.

PRESIDENT BUSH: Speaking of which, what happened with the Democrats, Karl. You promised me Joe Lieberman. Now it looks like John Kerry. Big difference.

SECRETARY RUMSFELD: All that goddam money we funnel to the Democratic Leadership Council and you couldn't even get us Gephardt?

KARL ROVE: There's only so much we can do. Howard Dean came out of nowhere and upset the whole show. It's going to be more challenging than we thought.

GOVERNOR SCHWARZENEGGER: I loved that scream though. What did you put in his drink?

SECRETARY RIDGE: That's on a strictly need-to-know basis.

SECRETARY POWELL: John Kerry also belongs to the Democratic Leadership Council. I might join myself.

KARL ROVE: Not so fast, Colin. We might need you to run for vice president.

VICE PRESIDENT CHENEY: Oh? And what am I? A potted plant?

PRESIDENT BUSH: I don't want to run against John Kerry. He's too tall.

SECRETARY RIDGE: Since 1900, the taller candidate has always won the election. You ended that with Al Gore. Sortof.

KARL ROVE: Just don't let him stand next to you during the debates. If there are any.

PRESIDENT BUSH: But Kerry was dumb enough to go over to Vietnam and get shot up. Three times. What is he, some kind of nut?

KARL ROVE: It's hard to understand. He could have bought his way out like you did.

PRESIDENT BUSH: Let's get something straight, Turdblossom. I didn't buy my way out of Vietnam. My Daddy did. I just wasn't dumb enough to go over there and get shot.

VICE PRESIDENT CHENEY: You had other priorities, George. We all did.

SECRETARY POWELL: Not all of us.

PRESIDENT BUSH: But the government was teaching people how to fly and Poppy flew and by God I learned too and look at all that's done for our country. It was God's will, for example, for me to fly onto that aircraft carrier to declare victory. Plus I really looked great in that flight suit.

ATTORNEY-GENERAL ASHCROFT: As you do again today, sir. It's all part of the Divine Wardrobe.

SECRETARY POWELL: Several hundred Americans and many thousand Iraqis have died since you declared "Mission Accomplished" in that flight suit, George. Question is, when do we get out?

SECRETARY RUMSFELD: I don't know, Colin. When do we finish draining their oil?

ALL: *Loud, prolonged laughter.*

KARL ROVE: It was undoubtedly God's will that you got caught with that cocaine back in the 1970s, George. If you had not been required to do community service, which interfered with your National Guard duties, who knows what might have happened?

VICE PRESIDENT CHENEY: Of course, we're all glad you were wise enough to duck your physicals.

PRESIDENT BUSH: That dental work was rough, though. I deserved a purple heart.

SECRETARY POWELL: Or a purple root canal.

SECRETARY RUMSFELD: All potentially damaging records of George's military service or lack thereof have been destroyed.

ATTORNEY-GENERAL ASHCROFT: Challenging George W. Bush's military record is an act of terrorism.

PRESIDENT BUSH: Well, yeah, but a lot of people are doing it. Things are really getting ugly out there.

SECRETARY RUMSFELD: And about to get uglier. I've seen the pictures.

KARL ROVE: This Valerie Plame thing for example. Our flaks ran with it when we outed her CIA cover. But I think there'll be some blowback.

SECRETARY RUMSFELD: We're also doing some, shall we say, diligent questioning of the prisoners at Abu Ghraib in Baghdad.

SECRETARY POWELL: Sooner or later, that kind of stuff always comes out.

KARL ROVE: The White House legal staff has prepared a brief showing that we are not bound by the Geneva Accords. Not at Al Ghraib. Not at Guantanamo. Nowhere.

SECRETARY POWELL: That'll do it for Fox, but I doubt it'll fly with the BBC.

SECRETARY RUMSFELD: Lets just make sure no visuals get out. I've set the guidelines. But I've seen the pictures. They are not pretty.

ATTORNEY-GENERAL ASHCROFT: Publicizing what's going on in our military prisons is an act of terrorism.

SECRETARY POWELL: This is America, Don. Sooner or later, one of our own people will blow the whistle. Maybe you should stop doing what you're doing.

ALL: *Loud, prolonged laughter.*

KARL ROVE: It's great having you around, Colin. Wanna be Vice President.

VICE PRESIDENT CHENEY: HEY!

PRESIDENT BUSH: I heard a rumor John Kerry's grandfather was Jewish. Do you think he's been circumscribed?

KARL ROVE: Ask his wife. She'll tell you. She'll probably even tell Fox. We're going to have a lot of fun with John's divorce file, too.

VICE PRESIDENT CHENEY: You're the master, Karl. Dick Nixon loved that stuff. Remember how you and me and Don Segretti and Gordon Liddy used to ratfuck the Democrats back when they ran McGovern. Then we'd slip the reports to Dick. How he'd howl!! Damn, I miss those days.

KARL ROVE: I do too, Dick. Then you took over Halliburton, I took over Texas, and now we run the world.

PRESIDENT BUSH: Me too! I run it too!!

VICE PRESIDENT CHENEY: So here it's 2004 and we're getting a raft of shit from all sides. None of which matters. The Columbia doesn't matter. Body bags don't matter. Baghdad and 9/11 don't matter. Deficits don't matter. Torture. The environment. The Democrats. John Kerry. They can all go fuck themselves.

KARL ROVE: We have a hard core 40% fundamentalist vote that will never leave us. George could drop his pants on national television and they'll still vote for him.

VICE PRESIDENT CHENEY: Be a little tricky to get him out of that flight suit, though. Ha ha ha.

PRESIDENT BUSH: The Haves and the Have-mores. That's our base.

KARL ROVE: We've got more money than God, and it's all well concealed. We've got the vote count rigged, especially in Florida. We're still bouncing the blacks off the voter rolls. If it's close, we'll roll out the troops. Blacks, Hispanics, hippie types…if think they're going to vote come November, they're dreaming. U\

PRESIDENT BUSH: Right. And if they think their votes are going to be counted, they don't know my brother.

VICE PRESIDENT CHENEY: We've got the media lined up. We've got Saddam ready for release. We've got Osama in October. A terror attack around election day. Scalia's got the court wired to call it all off if we have to. We'll let the Democrats think they've got us on the ropes. Then we slit their throats, just like 1972.

KARL ROVE: Right Dick. All the way down the line. But what makes you think you'll still be on the ticket?

TWENTY-ONE: March, 2004
"The Democrats are starting to think they can beat us"

PRESIDENT BUSH: Hey! Boy Genius! I thought you controlled the media. What am I hearing? What am I seeing? They're creaming us out there.

KARL ROVE: It's essential to let the public think there's a real debate going on. We can't shut the media entirely down. It would look unAmerican.

VICE PRESIDENT CHENEY: As unAmerican, lets say, as the fact that all the major media are owned by five corporations that answer to us. Ha ha ha.

KARL ROVE: It's a long way to November, George. Let em howl. It's their therapy.

PRESIDENT BUSH: Kind of like letting Ann Richards yell about Daddy being born with a silver spoon in his foot. Then, pow, we chop her head off. Damn, that was fun!

KARL ROVE: Exactly. It gives the liberals the illusion they have some power, and a chance to win the election. That way, when we blow them away in November, they'll be both disheartened and exhausted. Then we crush them for good.

VICE PRESIDENT CHENEY: I can't wait.

KARL ROVE: You may have to.

GOVERNOR SCHWARZENEGGER: I see a lot of people out there hating George W. Bush. You are not exactly popular in California.

SECRETARY RUMSFELD: Especially not with the girlie-men. Right, Arnold?

SECRETARY POWELL: Day after day we are accused of lying to the world.

GOVERNOR SCHWARZENEGGER: Yah. The Democrats even begin to think they can beat us.

ALL: *Loud, prolonged laughter.*

KARL ROVE: Lied? Lied about what? About the war in Iraq? Just because our neo-con advisors planned the attack ten years before 9/11? Just because we all knew there were never any weapons of mass destruction? Just because we didn't stop the Saudis from hitting New York on September 11, and then flew the bin Ladens out of the country? Just because Saddam hated Osama and vice-versa? Just because we crushed Afghanistan so we can build a pipeline? Just because we're trashing Iraq for their oil and never intend to leave? Just because we don't let anyone photograph the body bags coming home?: Just because George doesn't go to any military funerals? Just because we'll kill Saddam as soon as the time is right? Just because we'll surface Osama in October? Just because we use terrorism to burn that damn Bill of Rights? Just because we've made George W. Bush the most powerful instrument of God the world has ever seen? Just because everybody knows we'll cancel the November elections if we're losing? Is that why they say we don't tell the truth, Tom?

SECRETARY RIDGE: Our polls are dropping. Our approval ratings are down. We can't take too much more bad publicity.

SECRETARY RUMSFELD: Wait 'til you see the pictures from Abu Ghraib.

KARL ROVE: Or maybe it's the domestic stuff that has people bothered. Could it be that we've trashed the Social Security funds after promising to protect them? That we've run up the biggest deficits in world history after saying we'd balance the budget? That we've put up for sale every corner of the natural environment after promising to protect it? That we've trashed the educational system and bankrupted the states? That we blew up another shuttle while George rants about going to Mars? That "compassionate conservatism" has served as a punch line for a total assault on a popular legacy of social programs? That we're putting women and people of color where they really belong? That we're the first administration since Hoover to have fewer jobs at the end of our four-year term than before? That we're about to take charge of the Supreme Court and shred the Bill of Rights forever? Things like that. Do you think that's what's bothering people, Tom?

SECRETARY RIDGE: Well, yes, among other things.

ATTORNEY-GENERAL ASHCROFT: Don't forget stem cell research and the evils of contraception and abortion. These are also areas where we are doing God's will.

KARL ROVE: Well, let me tell you something, gentlemen. NONE OF IT MATTERS. It takes a focussed effort by the major media to sustain these issues. The five corporations that own America's airwaves all have clear vested interests. They all answer to me.

VICE PRESIDENT CHENEY: That was Reagan's Teflon. There was never any follow up. Scandals would break one day and disappear the next. Not like Whitewater.

SECRETARY RIDGE: The Whitewater investigation started with a small real estate deal and spanned the entire Clinton Administration. It resulted in his being impeached for lying about sex.

KARL ROVE: Right. Do you see anything like that happening with George here? Iraq, the WMDs, the breakdowns on 9/11, the deficits, the environment, the profiteering, Valerie Plame, you name it, it's up one day, gone the next. Poof! Magic!

VICE PRESIDENT CHENEY: I wish you wouldn't mention that profiteering stuff, Karl.

GOVERNOR SCHWARZENEGGER: Yah, it's very impressive how you make people forget what you want and remember what you want. Even in California nobody remembers it was Enron that crashed the economy. You made them think it was Gray Davis. That's why I am governor.

KARL ROVE: We will have our ups and downs, gentlemen. We had them in Texas too. But the media control what people think, and we control the media. It's as simple as that.

ATTORNEY-GENERAL ASHCROFT: We are anointed by God. Independent thought is an act of terrorist heresy.

SECRETARY RIDGE: But the ticket could still use shaking up.

SECRETARY RUMSFELD: When the photos from Abu Ghraib come out, there'll be a whole lotta shaking goin on.

VICE PRESIDENT CHENEY: Agreed. So what shall we do?

KARL ROVE: Well, Dick, how's that ticker of yours?

VICE PRESIDENT CHENEY: What?

GOVERNOR SCHWARZENEGGER: Heart. Your heart, *dumbkopf*.

VICE PRESIDENT CHENEY: It's fine.

SECRETARY RIDGE: Our files show otherwise.

SECRETARY RUMSFELD: Is that why you hid out during the 9/11 attacks. Afraid your ticker couldn't take the stress? Or just afraid?

KARL ROVE: We can't have that, Dick. We might need to make a change.

VICE PRESIDENT CHENEY: Who will run the country?

PRESIDENT BUSH: Me! I will!!

VICE PRESIDENT CHENEY: Oh, I see. Reading *My Pet Goat* while the towers….

PRESIDENT BUSH: HEY!!

KARL ROVE: No need to get testy, Dick. But our polls show Rudy Giuliani, John McCain and Colin here all running ahead of you.

VICE PRESIDENT CHENEY: I thought the whole thing was wired.

KARL ROVE: It is. But we never take chances. We never misunderestimate, as George would say.

VICE PRESIDENT CHENEY: Rudy's got that prostate thing.

ATTORNEY-GENERAL ASHCROFT: Mayor Giuliani has been divorced and had many mistresses. I don't think…

GOVERNOR SCHWARZENEGGER: Oh yah, that mistress thing. That will play well in California.

SECRETARY RIDGE: And New York.

VICE PRESIDENT CHENEY: We're not going to carry either one of those.

KARL ROVE: John McCain also gives us a big bounce.

PRESIDENT BUSH: Ooooh. John McCain. He hates me.

SECRETARY POWELL: Maybe you shouldn't have impugned his patriotism. He did spend five years in a prisoner of war camp.

PRESIDENT BUSH: Well, what do you think it was like for me at Yale?

KARL ROVE: I would venture to say that with John McCain or Colin Powell on the ticket we might actually win this election by conventional means.

SECRETARY RUMSFELD: You mean a fair campaign and an honest vote count? I believe that would send the wrong message, a message of weakness.

VICE PRESIDENT CHENEY: I agree. It's fair elections themselves that are the problem.

ATTORNEY-GENERAL ASHCROFT: We elected by God, not the heathen masses.

SECRETARY POWELL: I'm not sure this is a ticket I'd really want to be part of.

VICE PRESIDENT CHENEY: You know, Colin, there are some great openings at Halliburton for a man of your....

PRESIDENT BUSH: Hey! Arnold. It's time to go pump. Dick. Karl. Let me know when you work this one out. Come next term, though, I'm taking over.

ALL: *Loud, prolonged laughter.*

TWENTY-TWO: March, 2004
"Better bone up on your Cuban!"

KARL ROVE: Gentlemen, we have a problem.

PRESIDENT BUSH: This had better be good, Boy Genius. Your little emergency phone call here is costing me gym time. You know I don't go for that.

SECRETARY RIDGE: Mr. President, the bombs that went off in Spain killed some two hundred people. It's the worst terrorist attack in the history of Europe.

PRESIDENT BUSH: So?

SECRETARY POWELL: The entire continent is saddened and traumatized. These were ordinary civilians, with families. Some were children, even pregnant women. Spain has been at peace for a half-century. Blood was everywhere. It's a terrible human tragedy.

PRESIDENT BUSH: Karl, what are these two guys whining about?

KARL ROVE: We lost the election.

PRESIDENT BUSH: Oh. That's serious.

VICE PRESIDENT CHENEY: This was all timed out very carefully, George. Two days was just about the right gap before a national election. We figured the bombs would go off, the nation would go into mourning, be furious with ETA or Al Queda or both, and our hard-liners would sail in.

PRESIDENT BUSH: We've been over this a hundred times. What happened?

KARL ROVE: Well, we know you haven't had time to be briefed, George. And we didn't want to interrupt you in your bench pressing.

PRESIDENT BUSH: You better think about joining me, Fart Nugget. You look like you're pregnant again.

ATTORNEY-GENERAL ASHCROFT: Where's Governor Schwarzenegger. I thought he was lifting weights with you.

VICE PRESIDENT CHENEY: Arnold flew back to California for a secret meeting with Ken Lay. The Democrats sued Enron for $9 billion of the hundred billion or so they took from the ratepayers. We asked Arnold to find a way to kill the suit.

PRESIDENT BUSH: Kenny-boy's been through a lot. I understand he had to sell three or four of his houses. It just isn't fair.

ATTORNEY-GENERAL ASHCROFT: Some godless careerists in Justice want to indict him. Yet they ignore the real criminals, like the pot smokers and abortion doctors.

VICE PRESIDENT CHENEY: At least we got the Martha Stewart thing going. That's taken some of the focus off Enron.

KARL ROVE: After the election you can go after the real killers, John. Soros. Peter Lewis. Harry Bellafonte. Whoopi Goldberg. All those Hollywood creeps.

SECRETARY RUMSFELD: They're going to love it at Guantanamo. Especially after Martha does the decorating.

VICE PRESIDENT CHENEY: We can call it Hollywood South. Ha ha ha.

PRESIDENT BUSH: So what's all this got to do with interrupting my work-out?

KARL ROVE: Well, we got it wrong in Spain. We thought the bombings would result in a big backlash and a landslide for our people there. Instead, they turned the nation even more strongly against the intervention in Iraq. The new Socialist government says it's going to pull its troops out.

PRESIDENT BUSH: Are you losing your touch, Turdblossom? Maybe we should shorten your name to just Turd.

VICE PRESIDENT CHENEY: Especially with this talk of changing Vice Presidents.

KARL ROVE: Get a life, Dick. This set-back in Spain could really hurt us.

SECRETARY POWELL: Nothing has hurt us more than not finding those weapons of mass destruction.

SECRETARY RUMSFELD: Wait 'til you see the pictures from Al Ghraib.

SECRETARY RIDGE: What are you talking about, Don?

PRESIDENT BUSH: What happened to Plan B?

KARL ROVE: The Spaniards choked. They wimped out.

SECRETARY POWELL: Plan B? I'm sorry. Am I missing something here?

VICE PRESIDENT CHENEY: We had a two-pronged strategy. If the post-attack polls showed the Spanish public angry with the terrorists and shifting toward our people, we would let the elections go ahead. But if the polls swung the other way, the military would cancel.

KARL ROVE: There may have been a polling problem. They may not have had time to get the numbers together to make a decision.

SECRETARY RUMSFELD: That's B.S. They knew they were going to lose the election. They just didn't have the *cajones* to call it off. Or to rig the vote count.

PRESIDENT BUSH: Too bad Jeb's not governor there. He speaks Spanish, you know.

KARL ROVE: Well, they lost their nerve.

SECRETARY POWELL: I doubt the Spanish people would have stood for martial law, Karl. And the army probably would have stood with the people.

PRESIDENT BUSH: You don't think that could happen here do you?

SECRETARY RIDGE: A substantial majority of the Spanish army would have refused to fire on civilians. Many would have supported the new regime and gone AWOL.

PRESIDENT BUSH: Well in that case they should have been shot. You can't let people just walk away from their military obligations.

KARL ROVE: September 11 happened on the day of the New York primary. We had no trouble postponing the voting. We learned a lot from that.

VICE PRESIDENT CHENEY: But if we're losing come November....

KARL ROVE: Not gonna happen.

VICE PRESIDENT CHENEY: Maybe you're not the Boy Genius you once were. Colin tanked at the United Nations. George's State of the Union stank. Now you've blown Spain. Maybe we can replace you with, say, Rudy Giuliani, or Colin over there.

KARL ROVE: It's all in the timing. We assume that if we're down in the polls in October, a terrorist attack will turn those polls around. When Bill Casey and George's Dad delayed the Iran hostage release in 1980, we assumed a two week cushion. Carter's polls tanked about fourteen days before the voting. We knew once we got within two weeks of election day, even their release couldn't save him.

SECRETARY RUMSFELD: What a peacenik wimp Jimmy was. You wouldn't believe what Saddam said about Carter when Ronnie had me thank the Iraqis for gassing the Kurds and Iranians.

KARL ROVE: So if we time the terrorist attack two weeks before the election, that'll give us time to monitor the polls. If they go against us, we can still get the Supremes to call off the elections like they called off the Florida vote count in 2000.

SECRETARY RUMSFELD: Or we can just call out the army.

SECRETARY POWELL: Whose army?

VICE PRESIDENT CHENEY: That's what Dick Nixon was going to do in '72. McGovern turned out to be such a loser it wasn't necessary. But if Dick had been behind, he was going to nuke Hanoi two weeks before the vote. When the streets really went wild, he would've declared martial law and cancelled the election.

KARL ROVE: It's a testimony to the gutlessness of the Democrats that LBJ never even contemplated that in 1968. He actually thought he was going to get the South Vietnamese to agree to a peace treaty before the election so Humphrey could squeak in.

VICE PRESIDENT CHENEY: We killed that off at the last minute. Nixon called the Vietnamese personally to assure them they could expand their drug trafficking if they killed the peace talks so he could win the election. Then Dick declared the war on drugs and drove heroin prices through the roof. Those guys got incredibly rich.

KARL ROVE: We all did.

SECRETARY RIDGE: Technically, Richard Nixon's interference with President Johnson's secret Vietnam peace talks in 1968 was an act of treason. He could have been imprisoned, or even executed. Certainly tens of thousands of people died in the lengthened war.

VICE PRESIDENT CHENEY: Dick didn't mean to kill all those people. He just had other priorities.

ALL: *Loud, prolonged laughter.*

PRESIDENT BUSH: Better bone up on your Cuban, guys. We got another Florida vote count coming up.

SECRETARY POWELL: Are you lifting weights in that flight suit, George?

PRESIDENT BUSH: Yeah, it helps me sweat. Are you Vice President yet?

TWENTY-THREE: April, 2004
"Tony! Tony! Tony!"

PRESIDENT BUSH: Tony! Tony! Tony! It's great to have you here.

JUSTICE SCALIA: Good to be here, Mr. President. It's nice to be away from those stuffy Supreme Court chambers for a change. Clarence's videos, while exciting, do get repetitious.

KARL ROVE: We take care of the people that take care of us.

JUSTICE SCALIA: And I want to thank you again for that duck hunting trip, Dick. Not only did we shoot some birds, we infuriated the liberals, which always does my heart good.

VICE PRESIDENT CHENEY: No problem, Tony. Quack! Quack!

ALL: *Loud, prolonged laughter.*

PRESIDENT BUSH: You know, Tony. Without you, there'd be no George W. Bush presidency. And we may need you again.

ATTORNEY-GENERAL ASHCROFT: If not for the Supreme Court, the Good Lord would still be contending with that anti-Christ, Al Gore.

SECRETARY RIDGE: Antonin Scalia persuaded the Supreme Court to stop the counting of votes in Florida and thus to guarantee George W. Bush's victory in the 2000 election.

ATTORNEY-GENERAL ASHCROFT: The votes that weren't counted were all cast by Satan. We must eliminate them again this year.

JUSTICE SCALIA: The best part was when that Ginsburg woman went faint after Sandy O'Connor decided to vote with us. I still chortle with glee.

ATTORNEY-GENERAL ASHCROFT: God was with you.

KARL ROVE: Yes, and God seems to have put a few million bucks in each of five Swiss bank accounts.

JUSTICE SCALIA: Yes, and I thank you, and Clarence thanks you, and Bill Rehnquist thanks you, and Tony Kennedy thanks you. But I think Sandy is experiencing some guilt.

SECRETARY RIDGE: Justice O'Connor was the last to come around to stopping the Florida vote count. Apparently she had an agreement with Justice Ginsburg.

JUSTICE SCALIA: Women! You can't leave them alone. Sandy and Ginsburg were going to wait for more arguments, which would have given Gore a few more days, and thus the election.

KARL ROVE: We found ways to work Sandy over pretty good. Along with that fat check in that Swiss bank, the promise to let her live seemed to do the trick.

VICE PRESIDENT CHENEY: That horse's head in her bed didn't hurt either. Ha ha ha.

KARL ROVE: We still needed some serious street intimidation to stop that vote count. Gotta love my Young Republicans. They'll strike again if gets too close again.

SECRETARY RUMSFELD: Those Young Republicans worked well with the goodfellas Jim Baker hired. Who knows, maybe there's another Turdblossom among them.

KARL ROVE: A few, I know, were quite handy with the baseball bat.

VICE PRESIDENT CHENEY: And more than ready to hang a few chads. Ha ha ha.

JUSTICE SCALIA: I, too, am ready to serve again if needed.

VICE PRESIDENT CHENEY: We do appreciate your keeping me from having to testify about who drew up the Bush Energy Plan. Those drafts from Kenny-Boy and the Enron marketing department would not be helpful now.

JUSTICE SCALIA: Just remember the number of that Swiss bank account.

KARL ROVE: Billable hours from a Supreme Court Justice have quite a few zeroes behind them, don't they, Tony.

VICE PRESIDENT CHENEY: Not to mention that Chief Justice slot when Rehnquist goes bye-bye.

JUSTICE SCALIA: Which, by agreement, you'll be arranging soon enough;

PRESIDENT BUSH: I think we're ready for a few bye-byes on that Court after November. Starting with that damn David Souter. He tried to kill my daddy.

KARL ROVE: That was Saddam, George. David Souter merely betrayed us all by leaning liberal after your Dad appointed him to the Court.

VICE PRESIDENT CHENEY: David Souter has consistently refused to do what we tell him. Not like Tony here. Loyalty is loyalty.

SECRETARY RIDGE: Supreme Court Justice David Souter has surprised many by voting to uphold the First amendment and other precepts of the Bill of Rights.

SECRETARY RUMSFELD: David Souter may need to visit Paul Wellstone. Soon.

ATTORNEY-GENERAL ASHCROFT: Voting liberal on the U.S. Supreme Court is an act of terrorism.

PRESIDENT BUSH: Does Souter still fly commercial?

KARL ROVE: David Souter doesn't go much of anywhere. Besides, the private plane thing is getting a little stale and a little suspect.

VICE PRESIDENT CHENEY: I like how we took care of Athan Gibbs. Crushed him with an 18-wheeler. It's good to see our people operating with a sense of humor.

SECRETARY RIDGE: Athan Gibbs founded TruVote, which developed voting machines that produce a paper receipt and allow voters to track their ballots. His invention could make it virtually impossible to steal an election. Mr. Gibbs just died in a freak traffic accident.

KARL ROVE: The term freak merely describes the truck driver we hired to do him in.

PRESIDENT BUSH: Well, what about that damn turncoat, Dick Clarke

SECRETARY RIDGE: Richard Clarke was a counter-terrorism expert for many administrations. His revelations that we put invading Iraq ahead of fighting terrorism have been particularly damaging.

PRESIDENT BUSH: Why the hell didn't he just stay on American Bandstand. I liked him there, at least before the Beatles went weird. He doesn't seem to age, does he? Can we bust him for Botox?

KARL ROVE: Fox and Krauthammer and Rush are all trashing him. Dick Clarke will become sound and fury, signifying nothing.

PRESIDENT BUSH: Ooooh, that's from the New Testament, isn't it?

JUSTICE SCALIA: I like how you let Colin Powell and Condi Rice take the heat for Iraq. It reminds me how your father set up Clarence Thomas, George. Playing the race card is a truly great American tradition.

KARL ROVE: We've also neutralized Paul O'Neil, Joe Wilson and Richard Foster. Just find a little chink in their armor, feed some scraps to our media and let the piranhas feed.

SECRETARY RIDGE: Paul O'Neill, our former Treasury Secretary, quoted Vice President Cheney as saying "deficits don't matter." Ambassador Wilson warned that there were no WMDs in Iraq, so we outed his wife as a CIA agent. Richard Foster pointed out that we deceived Congress about the true cost of federal health care.

JUSTICE SCALIA: But I especially enjoyed what you did to Jessica Lynch.

VICE PRESIDENT CHENEY: We made that girl a poster child for our war. Then she told the truth about what actually happened over there. She even turned down a million-dollar movie deal. How ungrateful can you get?

KARL ROVE: That story we cooked up about her being sexually abused diverted all the attention. She opens her mouth again and America will hear a lot more about her it may not like.

ATTORNEY-GENERAL ASHCROFT: The Lord smites those who question His crusade against the infidels. Especially carnal women. The Lord gives us license to say whatever is necessary to destroy these agents of Satan.

KARL ROVE: Which is why we brought you here today, Tony. We may need some help in November.

JUSTICE SCALIA: We made it clear in 2000 that our decision to shut the vote count was not meant to stand as a precedent. I don't think we could get away with it again.

KARL ROVE: We're talking about stopping the vote count before the votes are cast.

JUSTICE SCALIA: You mean canceling the election? Are you that far behind?

KARL ROVE: We're not taking any chances.

JUSTICE SCALIA: There is no precedent for canceling a presidential election.

PRESIDENT BUSH: Well, find some and get back to us. I gotta go pump iron. I sure do miss Arnold.

ATTORNEY-GENERAL ASHCROFT: Oh yes, me too.

TWENTY-FOUR: May, 2004
"Dancing in the streets of Fellatio"

PRESIDENT BUSH: Alright, Turdblossom. You really screwed up this time.

KARL ROVE: I know George, the Iraqis are going nuts on us. The assassinations are getting out of hand. So are the bombings.

VICE PRESIDENT CHENEY: Those pictures from Al Ghraib are killing us. Wow. Who could invent that stuff?

SECRETARY RUMSFELD: Every media outlet that carried those photos needs to be shut down.

KARL ROVE: CBS, NBC, ABC, CNN will all pay a price. Fox and Clear Channel, of course, are under control.

VICE PRESIDENT CHENEY: Sy Hersh, you can count your days.

PRESIDENT BUSH: Whoa whoa whoa, guys. First things first. Why is David Souter still alive?

SECRETARY RIDGE: Supreme Court Justice David Souter was recently mugged. We know who did it.

VICE PRESIDENT CHENEY: Of course we know who did it.

JUSTICE SCALIA: We will never get a vote to cancel the fall elections with David Souter still on the Court.

PRESIDENT BUSH: That sonofabitch betrayed my Daddy.

VICE PRESIDENT CHENEY: Some things just don't go as planned.

PRESIDENT BUSH: Right. Like you said they'd be dancing in the streets in Fellatio.

SECRETARY RIDGE: That's Fallujah, sir.

JUSTICE SCALIA: When I put you people in the White House I was assured I would not have to deal with any more liberals on the Court. They waste my time. I want people like Clarence and Rehnquist around me. People who do what they're told when I tell them to do it.

PRESIDENT BUSH: Tony. Tony. Tony. I know. I know. I know. The contract was arranged. They just screwed up.

ATTORNEY-GENERAL ASHCROFT: Allowing liberal Supreme Court Justices to live is an act of terrorism.

JUSTICE SCALIA: You and I had a contract of our own, George. When I stopped the vote count in 2000 Karl assured me that four Justices would be gone from the Court by 2004. We named them. They're all still there.

KARL ROVE: You got your money for Florida. All five of you did.

JUSTICE SCALIA: You promised I'd be Chief Justice. Now you want me to stop an election.

PRESIDENT BUSH: Right now, Tony, George W. Bush is Chief of the World. That's me. You've done a lot for us. And you're about to do a lot more.

VICE PRESIDENT CHENEY: You know, Tony, we at Halliburton make a really nifty line of cement shoes. One size fits all.

KARL ROVE: Tony, how about next time Rummy goes over to Baghdad, you go with him. Just don't lose your head.

ALL: *Loud, prolonged laughter.*

JUSTICE SCALIA: A deal's a deal, George.

VICE PRESIDENT CHENEY: We had a deal with Izzadine Saleem.

PRESIDENT BUSH: Who?

VICE PRESIDENT CHENEY: Izzadine Saleem. We made him head of Iraq. Then he crossed us. Somebody blew him up.

JUSTICE SCALIA: It's time I got back to the Court. Clarence wants to review the evidence in the Playboy case. Again.

KARL ROVE: Get going on the election, Tony. John Kerry is breathing down our necks.

JUSTICE SCALIA: Clarence would like some of those prison sex videos.

PRESIDENT BUSH: Him and Ken Starr. I hear Ken still gets horny over the Monica report.

SECRETARY RIDGE: Mr. President, Colin Powell is here.

KARL ROVE: Better scoot, Tony. Colin has some funny ideas about the separation of the Executive and the Judiciary.

ATTORNEY-GENERAL ASHCROFT: We have no such problems with the separation of church and state.

VICE PRESIDENT CHENEY: Tony, tell Clarence I'll send over my Al Ghraib tape. And get us those briefs.

PRESIDENT BUSH: Hello, Colin.

SECRETARY POWELL: Was that Antonin Scalia ducking out the back?

VICE PRESIDENT CHENEY: Lighten up.

SECRETARY POWELL: I'm sure I saw Justice Scalia here. The Constitution is quite explicit on the independent judiciary. If a Justice of the Supreme Court were to meet with you, especially in matters that affect you directly, like the Energy Plan case, it would be a terrible breach.

PRESIDENT BUSH: Actually, Colin, what's back there are Saddam's Weapons of Mass Destruction. Why don't you go tell the UN?

ALL: *Loud, prolonged laughter.*

SECRETARY POWELL: I've come here to resign.

KARL ROVE: Right. And Rummy is going to work for Amnesty International.

SECRETARY POWELL: The lies have been bad enough. So have the fake terror alerts. But these torture and sexual abuse scandals are way over the line. I don't see this war in Iraq being winnable. And I simply cannot stomach any more.

VICE PRESIDENT CHENEY: Nobody gets out of here alive, Colin. Not in an election year.

KARL ROVE: We have plans in place for November. But the margins are thin and the resignation of a Secretary of State does not compute.

ATTORNEY-GENERAL ASHCROFT: The Geneva Conventions are obsolete in the sight of our Christian God. We will not submit to prosecution.

SECRETARY POWELL: I don't recall such photos of sexual abuse coming out of Vietnam. I don't even recall stuff like this coming out of Nazi Germany. And I haven't read that the Geneva Accords were rescinded. What have we become?

KARL ROVE: Well, we've definitely taken a hit in the polls, Colin. They're showing Kerry up now. But we're about to shoot about $2 billion in stashed Enron cash at him and it's got to be well concealed. So I'm as worried about the Geneva Convention as I am about the Kyoto Accords.

VICE PRESIDENT CHENEY: I've got an extra copy of the Al Ghraib video for you, Colin. It's in color.

KARL ROVE: We're about to blow out another tidal wave of smear ads, Colin. Are you with us, or are you a terrorist?

SECRETARY POWELL: I've been a proud member of the United States military all my adult life. We are the nation of Washington and Lincoln. Of Franklin and Jefferson. How can you sit there and quote me poll numbers when the proud heritage of a great nation is being dragged through the slime.

KARL ROVE: These things happen. A month from now, nobody will remember.

VICE PRESIDENT CHENEY: Of course, if it happened on Clinton's watch, we'd've buried him with it.

KARL ROVE: The neo-cons. Wolfowitz. Abrams. Kristol. They're going to take the fall for this, just like Tenet is going down for the WMDs. You're in the clear. Again.

SECRETARY POWELL: You're doing absolutely nothing to promote peace in the Middle East.

SECRETARY RUMSFELD: We haven't got the oil out yet, Colin. When they're dry they can have peace.

ATTORNEY-GENERAL ASHCROFT: Peace in the Holy Land is counter to God's plan. Armageddon has begun. The Anti-Christ must be defeated. The Jews must come to Jesus.

KARL ROVE: All the bad headlines in the world don't match a ten cent drop in the price of gasoline.

PRESIDENT BUSH: Prince Bandar is going to lower oil prices. He promised.

SECRETARY POWELL: It hasn't exactly been "Mission Accomplished" in Iraq, has it? You went in with too many lies and too few troops. Our people are being needlessly killed.

SECRETARY RUMSFELD: Iran is next, Colin. You can plan that one. We'll see how you do.

TWENTY-FIVE: June, 2004
"Looks like Kerry and Edwards"

PRESIDENT BUSH: Okay, guys. It's war room time.

KARL ROVE: Yep. Looks like Kerry and Edwards. Nothing we can't handle.

VICE PRESIDENT CHENEY: The flip-flopper and the teenager. Piece of cake.

PRESIDENT BUSH: Kerry is still too damn tall.

VICE PRESIDENT CHENEY: Just don't let him stand next to you during the debates.

SECRETARY RUMSFELD: What debates?

KARL ROVE: Our polls are in range.

ATTORNEY-GENERAL ASHCROFT: Our Christian soldiers are holding steady at about forty percent. Nothing will shake them.

KARL ROVE: You got that right, John. Look at all we've been through. The scandals. The allegations. Halliburton. Al Ghraib. The body bags. The 9/11 Commission. The explosions in Iraq. And still our polls are in range.

SECRETARY POWELL: I don't see how you think the Abu Ghraib sexual abuse scandals are behind us. The whole world is nauseated and screaming.

SECRETARY RUMSFELD: You should've seen Hillary's face when we showed those videos in Congress. I thought she'd lose her lunch.

SECRETARY POWELL: We look like a bunch of sick, lying, murderous psychos, killing and raping whoever we want for oil and

Christian fanaticism. Is this what you plan for a second term? If so, count me out.

KARL ROVE: Ok. How about the Vice Presidency.

VICE PRESIDENT CHENEY: Fuck you, Karl.

SECRETARY POWELL: I don't want to be associated with mass-scale military sexual perversion like the world has never seen. I don't want to be associated with the destruction of 225 years of sterling American pride. I don't want to be part of obliterating the world's oldest democracy. I don't want to keep telling one vile lie after another.

VICE PRESIDENT CHENEY: You know, Colin, we have all sorts of services we perform at Halliburton.

SECRETARY POWELL: I'm not afraid of you, Dick.

VICE PRESIDENT CHENEY: Is this all something you didn't know about before you signed on with us?

SECRETARY POWELL: I had absolutely no idea how deep this went.

VICE PRESIDENT CHENEY: Did you expect a warning label? Karl and I broke in with Dick Nixon. We did the dirty work for Donald Segretti and G. Gordon Liddy. Were you born yesterday?

SECRETARY RIDGE: There are some interesting new books about the Bush family and its ties to dirty Saudi oil. The Bush family is known for taking care of both its friends and its enemies. .

KARL ROVE: Then there's your son Michael's position at the FCC to think about. I doubt the Democrats would want to keep him on.

SECRETARY POWELL: I know John Kerry quite well. I'm sure he can find a place for Michael.

VICE PRESIDENT CHENEY: We at Halliburton also have a place for him.

PRESIDENT BUSH: You know, Colin, there might be a seat or two opening up on the Supreme Court soon.

SECRETARY POWELL: Really?

KARL ROVE: Absolutely. And what an excellent choice you'd be, Colin.

PRESIDENT BUSH: You know, Colin, in times of stress, I always like to consult my favorite philosopher, Jesus Christ.

ATTORNEY-GENERAL ASHCROFT: Amen.

SECRETARY POWELL: You mean the Sermon on the Mount?

PRESIDENT BUSH: The what? The Servant on the what?

SECRETARY RIDGE: The Sermon on the Mount was Christ's great speech about Peace and human fellowship. Many Christian fundamentalists seem not to have read it.

ATTORNEY-GENERAL ASHCROFT: The Sermon on the Mount is communist propaganda. Christ never said a word of it. It was written by Jewish conspirators to make Jesus look like pacifist and a leftist.

SECRETARY RIDGE: There are many who think he was both.

PRESIDENT BUSH: Mel Gibson and I just had a long prayer session about Jesus. Have you seen *The Passion*? It reminds me a lot of those pictures from Abu Ghraib.

KARL ROVE: Even John McCain is coming around.

PRESIDENT BUSH: Oooh. He hates me.

KARL ROVE: But he knows where his bread is buttered. He knows where the power resides. And that would be with me.

SECRETARY POWELL: So what do you want from me.

KARL ROVE: You can resign the day after the election. If there is one.

VICE PRESIDENT CHENEY: We're not counting on many black votes. But we'll need what you can bring. Plus the few white moderates that still think you have some credibility.

KARL ROVE: Set up a Swiss bank account. There'll be a nice surprise in it.

SECRETARY POWELL: I have several.

KARL ROVE: We know. Choose one.

SECRETARY POWELL: And then?

KARL ROVE: And then you are going to see this country transformed.

VICE PRESIDENT CHENEY: As Ronnie put it, 'You ain't seen nothin yet."

KARL ROVE: We have our work cut out for us. But we also have our plans.

VICE PRESIDENT CHENEY: We have a mountain of stuff on Kerry and Edwards and their wives.

SECRETARY RIDGE: We also arrange terror alerts whenever the Democrats appear to be gaining momentum. I get to choose the colors.

SECRETARY RUMSFELD: That damn Kerry. Throwing his Vietnam medals over the fence. I was there. Who does he think he is?

KARL ROVE: We have rigged voting machines, we have felon exclusion lists, we have police ready to stop blacks and Hispanics from voting. In the swing states, we count the votes.

VICE PRESIDENT CHENEY: We have played the Saddam card, and we have more like it. We can time his trial on an as-needed basis.

KARL ROVE: We have Osama in reserve for October. We have terror attacks and color-coded warnings when we need them.

SECRETARY RIDGE: I like those colors. They certainly grab the media's attention away from things we don't want covered. Look what we did to stop the bounce after the Democratic Convention.

KARL ROVE: We have unlimited, untapped, untrackable cash reserves from Enron, Scaif and Halliburton. We have unprecedented control over the major media. We have both houses of Congress and most of the judiciary, plus the governorships in the four largest states. We have infiltrated the Democratic Leadership Council. We can count on the Supreme Court, as we did in 2000. We can summon the military if need be.

SECRETARY POWELL: Awful cocky, aren't you Karl?

KARL ROVE: Not at all. I also know that we are the most divisive administration in US history. We're the first since Hoover to lose jobs. For millions of Americans the economy is in the tank. Our policies on everything from stem cell research to the environment to women's rights to secrecy to energy policy to education to Medicare and Social Security and you name it have so thoroughly angered millions of mainstream Americans as to render them incoherent with rage.

VICE PRESIDENT CHENEY: We've even alienated the moderate wing of the Republican Party.

SECRETARY RUMSFELD: Our unilateral military interventions have infuriated most of the world, as did our lies about the WMDs and Saddam's ties to Al Queda.

VICE PRESIDENT CHENEY: Not to mention that pipeline across Afghanistan.

SECRETARY RIDGE: We have gutted the American economy and wasted our advantages over the rest of the world. It's now virtually inevitable that China, India and the European Union will soon outstrip us in technological and economic might. By 2010, our general material standing in the world could rank us number four.

KARL ROVE: For these and a thousand other reasons, we are probably the most hated administration this nation has ever seen.

PRESIDENT BUSH: But I speak for God. I am His messenger and His vessel.

ATTORNEY-GENERAL ASHCROFT: Praise Jesus.

KARL ROVE: So that means we never go below 40%. All we have to win is a couple of percentage points, or sneak though a bad count like we got in 2000. Or call the damn election off if we have to. Which, believe me, we can do.

VICE PRESIDENT CHENEY: If we get a second term we will utterly shred the Bill of Rights. We will double or triple the prison population. We will disappear the entire center-left leadership in this country, and as much of the rank-and-file as we can accommodate. American democracy will become a contradiction in terms.

ATTORNEY-GENERAL ASHCROFT: We will lay barren the Earth for Christ's return.

KARL ROVE: Could we lose? Yeah, Colin. We could lose. But choose the wrong side, and God help you if we don't.

ATTORNEY-GENERAL ASHCROFT: Amen to that. Shall we enlarge the chapel at Guantanamo?

SECRETARY RUMSFELD: How about enlarging the ovens.

TWENTY-SIX: August, 2004
"It will be the apocalypse! Now!!!"

PRESIDENT BUSH: Ok, Boy Genius, what do we do now?

KARL ROVE: Everything is going according to plan, George.

PRESIDENT BUSH: Oh? Why am I running against Kerry and Edwards instead of Lieberman and Gephardt? Why didn't capturing Saddam put us over in the polls? Why are they still blowing people up in Iraq? Why wasn't there a police strike at the Democratic Convention like we planned? Why did the story about us flying the bin Ladens out of the country leak out? Why are gas prices still over $1.50? Why did that report on the deficits just surface?

KARL ROVE: Have you looked at the polls lately?

VICE PRESIDENT CHENEY: We're running about even with Kerry and Edwards. That means we're way ahead. I foresee no problem.

KARL ROVE: You'll notice you're still on the ticket, Dick.

VICE PRESIDENT CHENEY: You'll notice our 40-plus percent fundamentalist support is still rock solid. I suggest you keep it that way.

ATTORNEY-GENERAL ASHCROFT: Our Christian soldiers are holding firm for Dick Cheney. Praise Jesus!

SECRETARY RUMSFELD: Will Jesus be bringing a cardiac unit for you, Dick?

KARL ROVE: We are a scant few months from taking absolute power. We set the stage in 2000, took a giant step in 2002, now we're poised to finish the job.

ATTORNEY-GENERAL ASHCROFT: America is about to become the absolute Kingdom of God. George W. Bush is His messenger. Liberal heretics, prepare for Hell!

PRESIDENT BUSH: Don't' go singing on us again, John. Mom's not happy about that coffee table.

KARL ROVE: We have suffered through the most unimaginable sex and torture scandal at Al Ghraib and emerged without a scratch.

SECRETARY RUMSFELD: Damned impressive. The media seems to have completely forgotten. If it were Clinton, he'd've been crucified. Again.

SECRETARY POWELL: Those images of helpless Muslim prisoners being sexually abused by American soldiers will resonate through the Islamic world for a thousand years.

PRESIDENT BUSH: November is all we care about. Those people don't vote here.

KARL ROVE: We have seen Halliburton skimming huge profits from food and gas services and other scams in Iraq with barely a ripple on public opinion.

VICE PRESIDENT CHENEY: Much of that cash is now well concealed in our offshore accounts. It will come in handy---and untraceable---in October.

SECRETARY RUMSFELD: The Enron money is there too. We're talking billions.

KARL ROVE: We have run up unprecedented deficits that will bury Social Security. Medicare, Medicaid, public education, environmental protection....they're all finished.

SECRETARY RIDGE: Many moderate Republicans are deeply disturbed by the huge deficits we have created.

SECRETARY RUMSFELD: In the age of George W. Bush, "moderate Republican" is an oxymoron.

VICE PRESIDENT CHENEY: We are selling off the natural environment without anybody seeming to notice. The air. The water. The minerals. The trees. They've brought in a few billion. Not as much as Iraq. But every bit helps.

ATTORNEY-GENERAL ASHCROFT: We must strip the earth of its heathen vegetation so Jesus can come, as written in Revelations.

KARL ROVE: We have used the worst terrorist attack in US history to build our poll ratings. We emerged from the 9/11 Commission without a scratch.

SECRETARY RUMSFELD: Not if you really read their report. But who reads anything these days?

PRESIDENT BUSH: September 11 was our great trifecta, gentlemen. It salvaged our polls, helps us crush free speech, made me a war president. What more could we ask?

VICE PRESIDENT CHENEY: Another attack. Soon.

KARL ROVE: Maybe.

SECRETARY RIDGE: We let the Democrats get through their Convention in Boston. I didn't even get to play with the terror alert color codings.

VICE PRESIDENT CHENEY: You know, Martha Stewart can help you with those, Tom. She has excellent taste. Ha ha ha.

KARL ROVE: Spain showed us these terror attacks can backfire. We lucked out on September 11, but a second time around could be tricky. We've got to be careful.

SECRETARY RUMSFELD: The camps are ready for the protestors that come at us at our convention in New York City. Shall we shoot a few?

KARL ROVE: That'll depend on the polls.

VICE PRESIDENT CHENEY: I'm sure many of that rabble will enjoy Guantanamo.

PRESIDENT BUSH: I hope you've got a special cell for Michael Moore.

SECRETARY RUMSFELD: I'm not sure I'd call it a cell.

KARL ROVE: We've got Osama ready to come out too, though the lack of bounce from Saddam was discouraging.

SECRETARY RUMSFELD: Saddam still knows a lot more than you need known.

KARL ROVE: He will be taken care of. And Osama should give us a good week when we need it.

PRESIDENT BUSH: We got his people out of the country after September 11. He owes us.

VICE PRESIDENT CHENEY: And we owe him. But too many voters already expect his capture. So in terms of an October Surprise, we need some fresh ideas.

PRESIDENT BUSH: How about a big campaign to protect unborn feces?

ATTORNEY-GENERAL ASHCROFT: We will outlaw abortion after the election. All those doctors, all those pregnant women, they can join the pot smokers and the ACLU types in prison.

KARL ROVE: But right now the abortion issue doesn't net us anything. The gay marriage thing didn't help either.

VICE PRESIDENT CHENEY: We've escaped every major scandal so far. The WMDs, the non-existent nukes, the no Saddam-Osama connection, the fact that the Iraq attack was planned long before 9/11, me saying deficits don't matter, Karl outing Valerie Plame....none of it has stuck.

ATTORNEY-GENERAL ASHCROFT: Praise Jesus!

KARL ROVE: Praise Fox, John. Praise Clear Channel.

VICE PRESIDENT CHENEY: The computer vote machine rigging is still solid. Not too much threat from paper ballots this year.

KARL ROVE: The felon exclusion lists are under attack, but we'll still shed a few thousand black voters across the south.

PRESIDENT BUSH: Jeb's still governor, isn't he?

VICE PRESIDENT CHENEY: We still have plenty of troopers to scare off people of color and elderly Jews in key precincts. We have many files on Mr. Kerry and Mr. Edwards and Mrs. Heinz Kerry and whoever else we need to smear.

PRESIDENT BUSH: Do I still have to debate?

KARL ROVE: That might be a good day for a terror attack. Kerry is too damn tall. The minute you're photographed next to him is the minute we call Tony Scalia to cancel the election.

VICE PRESIDENT CHENEY: Even if we lose the election…

KARL ROVE: …which won't happen…

VICE PRESIDENT CHENEY: …we would still have two full months, from November to January, to finish the job. We could call out the army….

SECRETARY RUMSFELD: Good idea. That would certainly give new meaning to the phrase "Lame Duck."

VICE PRESIDENT CHENEY: That would give me time to move my Halliburton shares off shore.

ATTORNEY-GENERAL ASHCROFT: We can't have it! We can't have a return of the infidels. The Bible says…

KARL ROVE: I don't think…

ATTORNEY-GENERAL ASHCROFT: You could push the nuclear button, George. Jesus will finally come.

PRESIDENT BUSH: And I'll be in my flight suit, just as I am today.

ATTORNEY-GENERAL ASHCROFT: The Apocalypse! It will be the Apocalypse! Now!!!

...to be continued...

www.ingramcontent.com/pod-product-compliance
Ingram Content Group UK Ltd.
Pitfield, Milton Keynes, MK11 3LW, UK
UKHW041428180426
11947UKWH00007B/344